MEMORIES

OF THE

BRANCH DAVIDIANS

MEMORIES OF THE
BRANCH DAVIDIANS

The Autobiography of
David Koresh's Mother

by

Bonnie Haldeman

as told to Catherine Wessinger

BAYLOR UNIVERSITY PRESS

Cover Design: David Alcorn, Alcorn Design
Cover Photo: David Koresh at age 8. Photo courtesy of Bonnie Haldeman. Used by permission. ·
Interior photos, courtesy of Bonnie Haldeman. Used by permission.
Except the following:

Photo 25, courtesy of Paul Fatta. Used by permission.

Photo 36, courtesy of Mount Carmel Visitors' Center. Used by permission.

Photos 51–52, government exhibit in the Branch Davidian civil trial. Public domain.

Photos 20, 58–68, courtesy of Catherine Wessinger. Used by permission.

Library of Congress Cataloging-in-Publication Data

Haldeman, Bonnie, 1944-
Memories of the Branch Davidians : the autobiography of David Koresh's mother / by Bonnie Haldeman ; as told to Catherine Wessinger.
    p. cm.
  Includes bibliographical references and index.
  ISBN 978-1-932792-98-0 (pbk. : alk. paper)
 1. Haldeman, Bonnie, 1944- 2. Branch Davidians–Biography.
3. Waco Branch Davidian Disaster, Tex., 1993. 4. Koresh, David, 1959-1993. I. Wessinger, Catherine Lowman. II. Title.

 BP605.B72H35 2007
 299'.93–dc22
 [B]

                     2007022395

Printed in the United States of America on acid-free paper with a minimum of 30% pcw recycled content.

With gratitude to my dear mother and family,
and all the friends who have stood by and supported us
with their love and kindness through these years.

—Bonnie Haldeman—

TABLE OF CONTENTS

FOREWORD

I first met Bonnie Haldeman on the evening of February 23, 2001 in a Cracker Barrel restaurant in Waco, Texas. That restaurant, with its old-style American country theme, embodies for me Bonnie's warm down-home qualities.

I had participated earlier that day in a symposium hosted by the J. M. Dawson Institute for Church-State Studies at Baylor University in Waco on "New Religious Movements and Religious Liberty in America." It was my first trip to Waco, although I had written a long chapter on the Branch Davidian conflict with law enforcement agents in 1993 in my 2000 book, *How the Millennium Comes Violently: From Jonestown to Heaven's Gate.*[1] Dr. Stuart Wright, a sociologist at Lamar University in Beaumont, Texas made arrangements for some of the surviving Branch Davidians to come to Baylor and meet with the visiting scholars after the symposium was over. That was the first time I met Clive Doyle, Sheila Martin, Catherine Matteson, and other Branch Davidians, and the only time I met Clive's mother, Edna Doyle, who passed away later in

2001. I had already met David Thibodeau, one of the survivors of the fire, when he attended the 1993 meeting of the American Academy of Religion in Washington, D.C. The Branch Davidians agreed to meet some of the scholars at the Cracker Barrel for dinner, and David Thibodeau gave me a ride to the restaurant.

When David Thibodeau and I walked into the store, there was a long line of people waiting to get into the restaurant that reached nearly to the front door. The Branch Davidians I had met earlier were there as well as a smiling, lovely woman with red hair, who introduced herself as Bonnie Haldeman. She introduced me to her husband, Roy Haldeman, a handsome older Texas man. I was trying to place where I had heard the name Bonnie Haldeman. It sounded familiar from my reading, but I couldn't quite recall who she was. Attempting to figure it out, I asked her, "When did you come out of Mount Carmel?"[2] I was stunned when she said with a smile, referring to David Koresh, "I'm David's mother." I enjoyed having dinner with her that evening and found her to be a friendly Southern woman.

Bonnie Haldeman's Autobiography

In 2003 I was able to be in Waco on February 28 for the tenth anniversary memorial service for those who died in the ATF raid, and also for the April 19th tenth anniversary service for those who died in the fire and all who died in the 1993 conflict. While I was at the April 19th service I resolved that, if the surviving Branch Davidians in Waco permitted it, I would devote my 2004–2005 sabbatical to recording their life histories and accounts of their experiences with the Branch

Davidians, the tragedy in 1993, and events afterward. I drove to Waco in August 2003 to ask Bonnie Haldeman, Sheila Martin, and Clive Doyle if they would permit me to interview them and then work the transcripts into autobiographies for each of them. They agreed.

I went to visit Bonnie Haldeman in her home near Chandler, Texas over the Fourth of July weekend in 2004. I recorded five tapes totaling 543 minutes with Bonnie. Clive Doyle was also there, and he supplied information that supplemented Bonnie's accounts. They took me to visit David Koresh's grave in a cemetery in nearby Tyler and on that trip I recorded ten minutes of their comments. After the transcripts were worked into a manuscript, Bonnie made corrections and additions to the text. I returned to Bonnie's home in February 2006 to scan the photographs included in this volume and to interview her further.

Bonnie's oldest son was born on August 17, 1959 just before she turned fifteen. She named him Vernon Howell, giving him her father's first name and his father's last name, although she and Bobby Howell were not married. Although Vernon did not change his name to David Koresh until 1990 when he was thirty or thirty-one, Bonnie consistently refers to him as David. All the surviving Branch Davidians call him David even when referring to his early years when his name was Vernon Howell. When recounting her memories of her oldest son to me, Bonnie called him Vernon up until the time he was about nineteen years old. From that point on, she referred to him as David. I have included that shift in her son's name in Bonnie's autobiography. Nineteen was a major turning point for David emotionally, and marked his increasing focus on religion.

Bonnie lived, worked, and worshiped with the Branch Davidians from 1985 to 1991. Although she left the Branch Davidian community that was increasingly based at Mount Carmel Center, about ten miles east of Waco, Texas, she still considers herself to be a Branch Davidian. Bonnie lost fourteen grandchildren in the fire at Mount Carmel on April 19, 1993, including two babies *in utero*. She misses all of her grandchildren, David, his wives, and her friends.

Bonnie speaks in the cadences of a Texas accent. It is easy for me to fall into that rhythm of speech since it is similar to the accent of my native South Carolina. In organizing the transcripts of the audiotapes into this autobiography, I have corrected grammar while seeking to preserve Bonnie's speech patterns. I have added footnotes to provide context for Bonnie's narrative. This book is Bonnie Haldeman's story about her life and her oldest son's life, and her memories of her Branch Davidian grandchildren, their mothers, and friends, told in her own words.

Acknowledgments

I thank Loyola University New Orleans for a grant that paid for some of my travel to Texas. I am grateful to my parents for a gift that supported my sabbatical and paid for transcriptions and editing. I am grateful for the enthusiasm and involvement of my editorial assistant, Alanda Wraye, who did the initial copyediting of the transcripts, which I then worked into the manuscript. I thank the transcribers, Sarah Vandergriff and Sharon Orgeron, for their careful attention to detail, and Clinton Wessinger for converting the audiotapes into digital files. I thank Clive Doyle for permitting some of his words to be incorporated into Bonnie's account. Most of all I wish to express my appreciation to Bonnie Haldeman for her Southern hospitality when I have come to visit and for graciously and honestly sharing her life experiences.

Catherine Wessinger
August 7, 2006

Purpose of This Autobiography

The main thing I want to do is make people more aware of the true facts. I want people to know what type of person David was, and what kind of people were at Mount Carmel. I knew 90 percent of them. David loved people and truth. He wasn't the person the media say he was. The media say he was just trying to get into people's brains and they compare him to Jim Jones. I can't judge Jim Jones because I didn't know him, but there hasn't been much of a human side put to David or most of the other people at Mount Carmel. I would like people to understand where David was coming from, and where I'm coming from.

Bonnie Clark

Childhood

I was born September 8, 1944 in Bastrop, Texas, in an Army hospital, as my mother describes it. Daddy was in the Army, and I don't think he even saw me until I was about eighteen months old. I was the second of seven children. My brother was two when I was born, and I was followed by four more sisters and another brother.

We lived in San Antonio, Texas until I was about eight or nine, because my father worked at Kelly Field. Then we moved to Houston. His name was Vernon Lee Clark. My mother's name was Erline Smith Clark.

To hear my mama tell it, my daddy was from a bunch of Kentucky roughnecks, who wore guns and all that kind of stuff. Her mother was a Tillman from England and was a more refined, aristocratic type of person. She came from money, and Daddy's daddy was very poor. My mama was raised on a farm. My grandmother couldn't wait to move to town. Eventually she got to move to town.

Daddy got out of the Army when I was a little girl. He then worked at Kelly Field in San Antonio. Kelly Field was one of the Air Force bases there. I think it's been closed since then. We lived out in the country in a little town called Atascosa. I remember this place from when I was four years old. There was a canal running in front of our house. I went out to wash an apple one day and fell in and almost drowned. My mother heard me screaming and came out and saved me.

I remember helping my daddy dig a well. He dug it by hand. He donated part of his land to build a Seventh-day Adventist church there for us to meet in. There were several families that lived out that way, including my father's sister and her husband. Those are some of the earliest memories I have from when I was four years old.

My grandparents, Mama's mother and dad, lived close by. Daddy left the Army and tried farming. We were going to school. He was working in a bakery and different things. Eventually we moved back into town. We moved to Houston and he went into the construction business. He was a framing carpenter.

We didn't have a lot of money. We moved around a lot when I was a child. I don't think Mama and Daddy ever owned a house until they moved to Dallas.

Mama sent us to Seventh-day Adventist Church school most of the time. She always wanted us to have a Christian education.

Brothers and Sisters

I'm next to the oldest. I was close to Gary, my oldest brother, and Janie, my sister who is younger than me. The others all came along a bit later.

When we were kids we used to walk to the library in Houston. We all liked to read. That was the way we entertained ourselves. We walked about fifteen blocks to get there. We read a lot. We didn't get to go to many places. We didn't have a car.

When my brother was about twelve he went to San Antonio and stayed with my uncle and aunt for two or three years, because my daddy was a drinker. Gary ran away from home, I guess, and lived with my mother's brother and their family for a few years. He came back later and then joined the Navy.

Church

We didn't go to church a lot. My mother joined the church, but Daddy never did go. As a little girl I used to go to church with my aunt and uncle, Mozell and Johnny Davis, who were my daddy's sister and her husband. They took me to church, and I spent a lot of time with them when I was a kid. I liked them. We lived just up the road from them. They would take me to church and all the church functions. I was about the same age as my cousin, so we did a lot of things together. That's where I got most of my religious education, because mama didn't have a way to go to church. She went when she could, but it was hard for her.

School

In San Antonio I went to the first grade and second grade in a Seventh-day Adventist school. After that we moved to Houston, and Mama got us into an Adventist school. I think I attended third and fourth grades at the Adventist school. I went to public school in Houston for a couple of years. We moved a lot. The majority of my schooling was in Seventh-day Adventist schools, mostly in Houston.

During my childhood, I was always very shy. I didn't make friends easily. I remember in the first grade I used to think something was wrong with me because I had red hair and my name was Bonnie. I loved my Aunt Mozell and was very close to her. She is the one I would go to visit. I loved cheese and tomato sandwiches, and she always made those for me.

My mama and daddy took us to the lake fishing every once in awhile. We didn't do much except stay at home.

Since we were poor, Mama never had the money to pay our tuition, so when I was in the seventh grade in Dallas Junior Academy I worked in the kitchen at lunchtime. I helped in there, and then cleaned the restrooms in the evenings to help pay the tuition for myself and for my sister Janie. That's about the time I met David's dad. I was just thirteen.

Bobby Howell

I was visiting with a friend of mine from school. Her name was Roxie, and her sister lived in the projects in Houston. Roxie's mother lived out in the country, so Roxie often stayed with her sister, and I'd go spend the night with her. That's where I met Bobby. I started staying over there a lot with Roxie.

Bobby took me to school one morning. He was on his way to work, I believe. He had a pick-up truck, and he reached over and kissed me as I got out of the truck. The principal was walking up the street and saw us. He called me into his office and expelled me.

So I went to a public school and finished out the seventh grade. I think I even started eighth grade in Houston, but then Bobby and I wanted to get married, and my daddy wouldn't let us. It was a stupid thing for anyone as young as I was to want to get married. I think Bobby was about eighteen. They wouldn't let us get married. Anyway I ended up pregnant.

I was fourteen by then. I had Vernon a month before I turned fifteen. When I was pregnant, Daddy signed the papers to let us get married, but then Bobby backed out of it. We each have different sides to our stories. God had a plan for my life and Vernon's life, which didn't include Bobby Howell.

First Pregnancy

I lived with my mama and daddy while I was pregnant. I guess I had a pretty good pregnancy.

It hurt my mother and my daddy. They were just shocked when their little girl came up pregnant. I stayed with them, but I visited over to Bobby's house a lot. His mother, Jean Holub, was always very nice to me, and I was close to his sisters. We would go visit their grandmother. I stayed at their house a lot, and my mother helped me, too. After I had Vernon on August 17, 1959, my mother helped a lot with him. God bless my mama. I don't know what I would have done without her.

At that time, Bobby's mother's last name wasn't Holub, it was Smith. Virginia was her real name, Virginia Smith. Bobby was her oldest child. She was always very good to me, she was just a big-hearted woman. She took in everybody around the neighborhood. All the time that I was pregnant and staying at their house, Bobby had another girlfriend. He would bring her around and Jean would run them off.

I spent a lot of time there, but Bobby and I weren't having a relationship at that time. When I had Vernon in Herman Hospital in Houston, his mother came to the hospital, but Bobby never came to the hospital to see Vernon. He never supported Vernon or anything like that. Later we talked about getting married, but we never did.

August 16 was a Saturday or a Sunday night. Daddy wasn't home. He finally came home very late. He was drunk. My daddy was an alcoholic. I remember waking up about 2:00 or 2:30 in the morning and going to the bathroom. I had a stomachache. My mother kept hearing me go to the bathroom. She said, "Let me see what's wrong!" I said I had a stomachache and she said, "You're going to have that baby." She started trying to wake Daddy up and he didn't want to wake up. Finally about 6:00 a.m. we got him up and the three of us got in the truck. We lived in the Heights in Houston, and he drove us to Herman Hospital. Of course, he wasn't feeling too good. That was the roughest ride I've ever had in my life!

We got to the hospital about 6:30 a.m., and I had Vernon at 8:49 a.m. I remember that the worst part about it was when they bent me over the side of the table and did a spinal block. That hurt. They took me right on in. I remember they laid Vernon across my leg when he was born. You know, they lay the baby across your abdomen to cut the cord. He was crying. I thought, "He's my baby." It felt good.

They held him up and said, "You have a little boy." I stayed in the hospital for five days. I remember they came in and said, "You can go home but we can't let your baby go home. He's got a fever." I started crying. They said, "We're just kidding you. No, we're not going to send you home without your baby." That was when they didn't kick you out of the hospital twenty-four hours after you had your baby. You stayed several days.

I remember going home and wanting to get back into some clothes, which didn't fit. I walked up the street to use a neighbor's telephone, and it just wore me out. I didn't realize how tired I was.

I stayed with my mother and she helped me with Vernon. He had colic and cried a lot. He was several months old when I got on a bus and rode to my aunt and uncle's house in San Antonio. They had invited us to come stay with them.

Vernon Howell [David Koresh]

Vernon was special. He was such a cute little boy and just a sweet little thing, a pretty little baby. He had golden hair and dimples. He was a good little boy. My mother helped me a lot with him. I remember when Vernon was two I bought him his first little tricycle. He was so cute. I adored him.

When Vernon was still a little baby, about six or eight months old, I went to San Antonio and stayed with my aunt and uncle for a while. Bobby brought Mama down there to get me, and we came back with him. He wanted to get back with me, but that never did work out. We just never did get together.

I still had a relationship with Bobby's family during that time. I'd go over there a lot and stayed with them. His sisters and his mother and I were friends. I remember we were in the kitchen one day cooking. Vernon had the measles while we were there. I stayed in a dark room with him for three days.

When Vernon was big enough to be in a walker, I was cooking something on the stove, and I put the oven door down. He scooted across the room real quick and stuck his hand down on that hot oven door and burned his hand. That was traumatic. He cried.

When Vernon was four, I took him with me to Dallas, and Vernon never saw his father again until he was about nineteen years old.

I don't know what I would have done without my mother. Actually from the time Vernon was two until he was four years old she pretty much had him. By then I was working and I think I had moved to Dallas. I had met Roy [Haldeman] and moved, and Mother took care of Vernon, pretty much most of the time between two and four. It was during that time that my mother took Vernon to Sabbath school. He fell in love with Sabbath school as a little boy of four years old. He was such a good little boy.

When he was nineteen David [Vernon][3] looked Bobby up on his own. He started by looking for his grandmother Jean. Somehow by looking in a Houston phone book at all the

Smiths and Howells, he was able to reach Bobby's next oldest son. That is how he got Jean's telephone number and he called his grandmother.

This other boy must have been about seventeen or eighteen at the time, and he had never heard of David, but he gave him Jean's phone number. When David called Jean and told her who he was, she was just elated to hear from him. Over the years they had tried to find out where we were, but I didn't want them to know. I had started a new life. One of Bobby's sisters had lived right down the street from my brother, but they never told them anything.

Jean was very happy to hear from David. After that David went to Houston and met his father.

David was about nineteen when he looked them up, but I think it was still quite a while before he went and met them. David had more of a relationship with his grandmother. Bobby sort of stayed in the background.

Bobby comes to the memorial every year on April 19.[4] He regrets a lot.[5] Of course, we all grow up with regrets about what we did when we were younger. Jean came to the memorials, too, until she died about five years ago.[6]

Bonnie Out on Her Own

When Vernon was about two I met this guy named Joe. Actually I was with Bobby's sister one night, and she was with her boyfriend, and we went to a drive-in restaurant and there we met Joe. He had just gotten out of prison. We started liking each other. It wasn't very long before he wanted to get married. I told Bobby about it and he begged me not to marry Joe, but I did. I was married to Joe for about a year, two years maybe. Vernon came and stayed with us, but that didn't work out. Vernon cried a lot, and Joe spanked him a lot. That was when my mother got Vernon. She started taking care of him because Joe spanked him when he cried. I divorced him. I don't usually give Joe's name. He hasn't been in the picture in a hundred years. That's all I'll say. His name was Joe. That was a big mistake. You make a lot of mistakes when you're young.

Joe and I were together about a year and a half, and it was up and down, up and down, up and down. He eventually broke his parole and they picked him up and put him back in prison, so I never saw him again after that.

Joe sent a buddy of his who had gotten out of prison to find me and Joe wanted me to stay with him until he got out. I didn't know the guy from Adam, but indirectly that's how I met Roy.

Meeting Roy Haldeman

Bobby had an aunt, Joyce, and I heard she was working as a waitress at a lounge over on Canal Street, so I went over there one night to see her. It just happened to be the lounge that Roy owned, called the Jade Lounge.

When I first went there, Roy wasn't there. He had a partner named Doris. Roy called later on and Doris told him, "We've got a pretty little girl here who just came in," and he said, "Well, put her to work." He said he would be in later that night. I met him that night.

My friend Joyce lived upstairs from Roy in the same apartment complex. I was staying with her. I had an apartment of my own, but my sister was staying with me, and there was another couple staying there, too. They had my car. When I was visiting Joyce, before I stayed with her, some guy came over, took my car, stole it, and wrecked it. So Roy went over to move me out. We got to be friends. That's how I met Roy, and I did go to work in the lounge for a short time.

That's when he fell in love with me. All his friends told him it was a mistake, but he fell in love with me. He was from Wylie in the Dallas area. He took me up there to meet his family. We went up to meet them, and he sold his part of the club to Doris. He was thirty-four and I was eighteen. He was a *handsome* guy. He had been a seaman for seventeen years. He never did ship out after I met him.

The guy my former husband had told to take care of me until he got out of prison was named Danny and he came looking for me at Roy's club. I was scared of him. Danny came into the club right after I met Roy and wanted me to go with him. Roy told him to get out, that I didn't want to go, and to just leave me alone. Danny left, and we went to another private club, and he followed us there. Roy put me out the window in the back, and we took off and got away from the guy. I never did see him after that. Roy was sort of my knight in shining armor. He rescued me.

I had a lot of fun with Roy. We went to El Paso. We always liked to get out and drive to places and do things. Before we left Houston we did a lot of partying. Roy owned the lounge, so we had the nightlife. We would go to Dallas and go out with his brother-in-law, his brothers and sisters. That was before I got back in the church. Of course, all during that time I had been away from the church.

THE HALDEMAN FAMILY

Making a Family

Roy sold his share of the lounge and we moved to Dallas. We had been in Dallas about eight or nine months when I came home to Houston, got Vernon and moved him back to Dallas with us. He was five then. That's about the time I got pregnant with Roger, who was Roy's first son. I had Roger just before Vernon turned six. Vernon was going into the first grade when Roger was born.

All the time that I was pregnant with Roger, we lived on White Rock Drive in Dallas close to White Rock Lake. Whatever I told Vernon to do, he would do it. I could trust him. You know you worry about most five-year-old kids. I would say, "Don't go out the yard now!" and he wouldn't. He was just a pretty little boy, a good little boy, mischievous at times. I remember my mother told me that one time he filled up her gas tank with a water hose. He was playing like he was putting gas in the car.

Vernon always talked. He was a talker. He would ask me questions. He always wanted to figure out how things worked, even as a little boy. He made up little stories to tell and play. All the women who ever met him—my sisters-in-law, mother-in-law, every female that ever met him—just fell in love with him. He was so cute and sweet.

Vernon got on Roy's nerves though. Roy had never had any kids before. Vernon would always talk a lot, and he'd cry when I'd leave him in daycare. Roy would tell him not to cry, "Be a man!" Roy was always sort of stern with Vernon.

Roger was born July 4, 1965 on a Saturday night. I had not even had any pains yet. We were watching *Gunsmoke* on Saturday night about a quarter to ten, and I went to the bathroom. I had a little show. I thought, "Uh oh, I'm probably going to have the baby tonight." He was born at 12:04, July 4.

I told Roy and Jackie, Roy's sister who was living with us, "I think I'm going to have to go to the hospital." It took a few minutes before it dawned on Jackie what I had said, and then we all got in the car. My suitcase was packed and we drove to Garland Memorial Hospital. We got there about 11:30 p.m. The nurses got me in a room. While Roy went out to get my suitcase, they took me to the labor room. This was a small hospital. They called the doctor to come in. The doctor got there about 12:00 and started scrubbing up. The nurse told him, "You better hurry, doctor. Get down there and do your business. This baby's coming." It was really quick.

Roger was such a pretty little boy. I just loved to sit and hold him and rock him. Roy was proud of him. He was a really cute baby.

Roy and I married when I was six months pregnant. Before that we had been together several years, and I was close to his family, so it was like being married to him.

I had a really good pregnancy with Roger. I never had morning sickness or anything. Even with Vernon I had a fairly good pregnancy. I felt good most of the time.

Roy was as tickled as he could be. He only made a hundred dollars a week, so we didn't have a lot of money. At the time I got pregnant, Roy was working for his brother-in-law who had bought a gas station. Then his brother-in-law, Joe True, who was a union carpenter, started mentoring Roy and helped him get his union card to be a union carpenter. He got more pay then. I remember it was rough for Roy. He would come home and say, "Honey, I didn't know what I was doing today." But Joe was a good teacher, and Roy would always study things out and didn't get rattled. He worked at that until he retired.

We had a few little incidents. I was going to leave him once when I was pregnant with Roger. Even though Roy was tickled to have a child, he had been single for years and didn't realize he could not just get in the car and go anywhere he wanted to. I was doing waitress work at Howard Johnson's restaurant and leaving Vernon with my sister-in-law. I came home one night and Roy wasn't there. It turned out that he and his brother-in-law had gone to Houston. It made me mad so I moved out. I packed my car up and moved out. Roy came back, and he was very unhappy. He got home and we weren't there, so he found me at my sister's place. He was very mad, but I went home with him, because I was pregnant.

We rented a really nice house in Richardson on Plano Road. Buck, Roy's youngest brother, and his father-in-law were leasing land and farming it near Richardson. So we rented the farmhouse on the property on the edge of Richardson. Roger, I think, was two weeks old when we moved there. We lived there for seven years. Roy's sister Jackie lived with us for a couple years. She helped me a lot with the boys.

The Boys' Childhood Years

Things were pretty uneventful in Richardson. Vernon and Roger were kids. They played a lot and had fun. The house was in the middle of a wheat field, and they really were living the life of country boys, just having a good time.

After we moved out to the country, we'd have Vernon push Roger up and down the driveway in the stroller. Vernon told me one time, "I hope you don't have any more babies,

Mama." He didn't want to push any more. Roger was such a little clown.

Vernon started first grade. I think he had three different teachers that year. He failed first grade, so he was in first grade two years. By the second grade I think they were realizing that Vernon had some kind of learning disability. By the third or fourth grade, the school was having us do a lot of testing, and we were told that he had what they called a learning disability. It was not dyslexia. It was called a language disability. Kids who have this disability have high IQs, but they just can't get certain things. So the Richardson school district, which is a very good school district, put him in some special classes along with quite a few other kids.[7]

Vernon and Roger had fun growing up. Vernon loved to fish. They'd play. Vernon learned to work on lawn mowers. We had a barn that the boys played in.

When Roger got big enough they started sharing a room. They would laugh and giggle and play every night. Roy would send them to bed and have to get tough with them and make them hush and go to sleep.

We went camping a lot. Vernon loved to sit around and make up all kinds of scary stories to tell everybody. He was always doing something: building a little fort, building a little playhouse, working on his bicycle. He was just always into something. He was a very curious kid wanting to know everything.

My mother had taken Vernon to Sabbath school when they were still in Houston. That was when he was four, about the time that I brought him back to Dallas to live with me. He said, "Mama, I'll never forget. I remember the room and walking up stairs." They called the room "cradle row." It's the kindergarten for the little kids. He said, "Oh! That room was so pretty, Mama. It had flowers in it and all kinds of toys. It was just beautiful." He said, "I fell in love with Sabbath school." He did.

Vernon always loved going to church. When he came to live with me, we didn't go to church much for a few years. Vernon was nine, so Roger must have been about three when I started taking them to church. When Vernon was ten and Roger was four, we started going to church in Richardson. Vernon loved going to church. Roger didn't.

We came home from church one time, and Roy told Vernon to go out and cut the grass. Vernon said, "Daddy, I can't do that. This is the Sabbath." Of course, the Sabbath on Saturday was something new for Roy. He wasn't used to it. We were doing what we believed to be right on the Sabbath day, and Vernon took to it just like that, but we had to train Roy a little bit. Roger, he's just Roger. He didn't have too much interest in it. He enjoyed going to church, but not like Vernon.

Vernon met a lot of friends at school. He made friends very easily, and a lot of them would come out to the house. I think I gave him several birthday parties. Roger was born on the Fourth of July, so we celebrated on that day.

There was almost six years' difference between Vernon and Roger's ages. Once Roger got big enough they got along pretty well. They used to drive me crazy, aggravating me. They'd giggle and laugh and play instead of going to sleep like they were supposed to.

Family and Work

I think I went back to work when Jackie was still living with us and taking care of the kids. I was doing waitress work for a while. Jackie and her husband got back together, and they were both staying with us until they rented a house. Then I went to work at Texas Instruments, and one of my sisters came and helped with the kids. Then I went to school to be a manicurist and my mother took care of the kids. I took them over to her house in the mornings.

I was very close to Roy's mother. We did a lot of family sort of things. My mama and daddy lived close to Denton. We'd go out there. Those were some pretty good years. We just did things that families do. I'd take the kids to the lake on the weekends and feed the ducks, and they'd ride their bicycles.

Vernon's Adolescent Years in Sachse, Texas

In 1972 we bought our first home in Sachse. Roger was seven, so David must have been about thirteen. We moved to Sachse and, as a matter of fact, that's when Vernon started wanting to go to church school. Roger would have been in first grade, and Vernon was in his seventh grade. So I enrolled them in church school. Roy had a hissy fit: "We've got public schools all around here, and you have to take them over to ride a bus from Richardson." Anyway, I usually got my way. I took them. I had a friend, Barbara Mather, and we took turns driving our kids to catch the bus. We lived in Sachse, and she lived between Sachse and Richardson. I had to take the kids all the way to Richardson and they would catch the school bus, which took them on in to Dallas. It wasn't a big deal. I worked in that area a lot.

During the years before that, I was a manicurist in Dallas. By the time the boys started church school I was making new homes ready for showing by the builders. These were the homes that they had built. I'd get them ready to show by cleaning them up. I took the kids over to Richardson to catch the school bus on my way to work, and then I'd pick them up in the evening on the way home. I had a station wagon. Vernon and Roger were embarrassed because I had ladders on top of my car. I'd say, "Well, that's my job."

The boys went to church school for two years. Roger did very well in first and second grade, and David made a lot of friends. They did very well over there. We took the Mather boys with us to catch the bus one week, and the next week Barbara drove them over and brought them back.

Vernon had his first girlfriend at that school. Her name was Mary. She was a Spanish girl. He was really crazy about her. Roger's best friend was her little brother. We used to visit a lot between our homes. For a few years we were really big into church with a lot of activities. Roy even went with us a few times.

When David was about fifteen he wanted to take driver's education, and they didn't have that at church school. He wanted to go to Garland High for that, and so I took them out of church school and put them in public school in Garland. Vernon took driver's ed and he joined the football team. He dropped out of football because he didn't like the coaches' attitude. For them it wasn't just a sport. They'd say, "Get out there and kill 'em!" There was cursing. Vernon didn't like that, so he started running track. He didn't like the competitiveness of football.

Roger got into baseball and football. He did very well. Roger loved baseball, and he was on a very good team for baseball and football.

So for the next few years it was hauling the boys back and forth between track and baseball and everything, and that is about the time that Vernon started getting interested in religion.

Vernon always loved fishing. From the time he was a little boy, even when we lived on Plano Road in Richardson, he loved fishing. Fishing became really important to him when we moved to Sachse. My daddy was a fisherman, too. Vernon got into buying his own reels. He had to have a Garcia fishing reel and his own tackle box.

I bought Vernon his first guitar, a cheap one, but it was a guitar. He wanted to be a rock star. Then he had to have a better guitar, so I bought him a better guitar. I arranged for him to take some lessons in Garland at the music store, but he didn't take them very long.

So Vernon was into rock music, guitar, and fishing. Roger was into football, baseball, playing pool, and bowling. Roger was good at everything like that. There was a little place in Sachse called the Coffee Cup. It was not a drinking place. Roger played pool there and won trophies. I've got boxes of trophies that he won. He was into those kinds of things.

Vernon got interested in religion. He started listening to the radio preachers, and he started getting interested in girls.

I was working all the time, having problems with Roy, and Roy was working out of town. Time just goes by so fast it is hard to remember everything. I worked cleaning houses all the time. We were just living and doing things.

My parents were living in Tyler, Texas and Vernon wanted to go to school there. We let him do that for a while. He may have been there for a month or six months.

We lived in Sachse for seven years. During that time in Sachse, Vernon was into music, guitars, and all this kind of stuff. He was going to school.

I bought Vernon a truck. The first thing he did was take the truck bed off of it. That made me mad. "Mama, I want to redo it. I want to build my own back. I don't want that bed on the back of it." He was always redoing something we bought him. It was aggravating. We didn't understand why he kept doing that.

Vernon was never into drugs and drinking that I know of. The seven years, '72 to '78, were growing up years in Sachse.

David Thibodeau said in his book that David said that I beat him black and blue on his thirteenth birthday.[8] I got to thinking about that. I never beat him black and blue, but I might have whopped him once because he was being so bad that day. He was being so hateful, but I can't remember why.

Vernon hated to get his hair cut. It was always such a battle. Vernon was growing up in the '70s, but to Roy and me long hair was a symbol of everything bad. We were totally against it, and, of course, Vernon loved long hair. I remember the last time I took him to get a haircut, I swore I'd never do it again. He never made his son, Cyrus, get his hair cut.

As Vernon got older, he seemed to be more into religion, and he was having a hard time emotionally.

Vernon's First Serious Love and a Fight with Roy

Vernon met Linda when he was about seventeen. They went together. He spent a lot of time at her house. He wanted to marry her.

Vernon dropped out of high school in the eleventh grade. He went to work with Roy in Denton. He had a good job. We cosigned for a brand new Chevrolet pick-up truck. I think he made two payments on it. I went over and found him at Linda's house and he hadn't been to work.

David admitted to me years later that when he was about eighteen he set fire to his car (not the new truck) intentionally. He was having a hard time. I don't really know why.

Before we moved from Sachse, one day I went down to my neighbor's house at the end of the road to a Mary Kay cosmetics party. Vernon wasn't working. He was lying on his bed asleep. Roger came home from school, and we had a letter in the mail. Roy got the letter out of the mailbox and it was from school saying Roger was failing; he had been talking in class again or something. Roy had been drinking when he got home, and he jumped on Roger to teach him a lesson. They were out in the garage. Roy got his belt off and Roger was screaming bloody murder and woke Vernon up. Vernon ran out there to defend Roger and he hit Roy. It was a reaction. He always hated, and we all hated, Roy's drinking. If it had been a different situation it probably never would have happened, but it did, and Roy held a grudge against him for that for years. Vernon was reacting and maybe he shouldn't have hit Roy, but that's the way Roy could be when he was drinking—not that he beat anyone all the time—Roger probably needed a lot more whippings than he ever got—but that is the way it happened.

That's why David always taught later on, "Don't let me ever catch any parent disciplining their kids in anger. You can spank on their behiney—that's what it's made for—with paddles, but don't let me hear you discipline in anger or raise your voice, and let the child know what you're punishing him for."

I used to get mad at Vernon and holler and scream, you know like mamas do, and I probably whopped him too hard a couple of times. So he learned, and he took a lot of things he learned from everything we did into teaching his wives and children the proper way to do things.

Bonnie and Roy Move to Chandler: Transitions for David

When David was nineteen, somewhere around 1978, Roy and I were going down to my mother's house near Chandler and we passed a little country-looking house. I said, "Oh, that's a cute little place." My mother called me about a week later and told me it was for sale. We bought this house in October of '78.[9] Roy quit his job and started working on it. We didn't move until the following June of '79.

When I moved to the Tyler area I was looking for work, so I went to a house where a man, Dean Snell, and his son were working. They were trimming out the house, and I told them that I cleaned new construction. He said, "I'm not the builder here. I don't know if he needs anyone or not, but my wife manages some apartments, and I think she needs someone to clean the apartments." I met Helen Snell and started cleaning apartments when people moved out. In the meantime, Dean had built houses in Dallas, and they moved back to Dallas. She gave me a beautiful couch and all sorts of stuff. They really liked me I guess.

About a year later Helen called. She said, "We're living at Twin Oaks and Dean's been building for David Wilkerson. We've been building a new house for him. We'd like for you to come and clean it." It was just several miles down the road so I said, "Okay, sure." David Wilkerson is the evangelist who wrote *The Cross and the Switchblade*. He operates several organizations: World Challenge, Teen Challenge, and Youth Crusades.[10] It was a huge house. Dean and Helen Snell were living in a mobile home on that property.

I was working there and took my sister Beverly with me several times to help clean windows and everything. They knew I did good work. One day, Ron Porche, their business manager, asked me if I would like to clean their offices two or three times a week in the afternoons. I said, "I guess I could." I started cleaning their offices about three times a week. Then one day David Wilkerson stopped by and asked if I could clean house for him. So I cleaned his house. They had moved into the house, which was going to be an office later on, and they started building a bigger house in the back and an office right next to that. Little by little they were building more buildings. My work there evolved over several years. I was cleaning all their new construction, I was cleaning the offices, and I was keeping house for Brother David and Gwen a couple days a week. He paid me very well, plus a tank of gas a week. They were really nice. They were good to me.

Right before we moved to Chandler, my daddy had come up to Sachse and was working there. When we moved to Chandler in June '79, David didn't move with us. He stayed in Sachse and was working with his grandfather. I think David was living in his car at that time. Linda had already gotten pregnant, and her dad was mad and wouldn't let them get married. It really upset David, because he wanted to marry her. He loved her. Anyway, he stayed around the Sachse-Wylie area, and stayed with different friends, and then he came to Chandler and stayed with us for a while.

David had made a friend in Tyler, Harriet, at the Adventist church. He had known her when he went to school there while staying with my mother. He spent a lot of time at her house and at church. He was having emotional problems about Linda because she was going to have his baby and her dad wouldn't let them get married. He was going to church and studying the scriptures and wanting to do the right thing. The deacons in the church told him, "You'd be better off, just forget her." He said, "I want my baby. I want to support it."

Linda's father wouldn't let him see her again. David was decking houses in Garland. I went by his job one day with my sister-in-law, whom I was visiting. Linda came out there, too. I think that was before she had the baby. I had called her and told her I was going to be there.

Linda had a girl. David never actually saw Shae. I saw her when she was two weeks old. Shae was his first child.

Later, after David came to stay with us in Chandler, he started going to church in Tyler and staying with Harriet. She was a big influence on him. I think he was struggling. He told me he used to go to the graveyards and pray. He said that when he was in Sachse he would go and talk to different preachers. As a matter of fact, David went to talk with our neighbor across the street in Sachse, Billy Harrison. I guess he was questioning a lot of things, studying a lot of things, hearing a lot of things, and he was just trying to learn and he was frustrated. He went to church.

A few episodes happened at the church, because David was so zealous about the things he learned. He said he had a vision about the Holy Spirit being feminine.[11] I wasn't there, but he got up one night at the chalkboard and drew an outline of stuff and it just offended everybody at the church.

David was talking with Harriet because he was frustrated. He was learning things, and he was studying, and he didn't have any answers. Every time he'd ask questions at church everyone would tell him, "Shut up, Vernon. Listen. Don't talk so much. Listen."

One day David asked Harriet, "We're reading the Bible about all these prophets. Where are all the prophets today?" That's when she told him about Lois Roden and the people at Mount Carmel. Harriet said, "There is supposed to be one over close to Waco." Her mother had been Shepherd's Rod in California when she was a little girl. She remembered all the *Shepherd's Rod* books.[12] I think she knew Perry Jones, who lived at Mount Carmel, from her California days. Perry Jones later became David's father-in-law. David said, "I want to go see. I want to go meet these people." She said, "I'll take you."

VERNON HOWELL BECOMES A BRANCH DAVIDIAN

Early Visits

In 1981 David and Harriet drove from Tyler to Dallas, and then down to Waco. They didn't know how to get to Mount Carmel, but they finally found it.[13] They were there very late, until the wee hours of the morning, and they came back. Lois Roden invited David to come back.

I believe Lois Roden invited David to come visit and learn and study, so he went back. He was there several weeks, so Harriet and I went to visit. It must have been on a Sabbath. The church was still at the front of the property, so we pulled in there. There were a few cars, and people come out. I remember meeting Catherine Matteson, and a little Australian lady who never shut up [Edna Doyle, the mother of Clive Doyle]. I couldn't understand what she was saying. That's about the time of year my allergies started bothering me, and my ears would plug up, and here I was trying to understand what this lady was saying. I remember Clive Doyle standing in the background. He didn't say much. He was sort of aloof. I remember Catherine talking about how people were being cloned. Even then she came up with some weird ideas.[14] They had already had the early meeting. We went down to the Administration Building and had a potluck lunch. Later on it burned.[15]

I enjoyed it. Everything was simple. I just sort of fell in love with everyone the first time I went down there. I liked the way they lived and what they stood for.

Lois might not have been there at that time for some reason. I remember David taking us into her house. He showed me all the work he had been doing fixing things up. I went back several times after that.

David used to come visit me and tell me about all the things he was learning at Mount Carmel, for instance, Isaiah. He would just talk and talk and talk and talk. I didn't know what he was talking about. I was raised in the Adventist church and went to Adventist school and I still didn't know all those things. I learned more after David went to Mount Carmel. He would come back and teach me more than I had ever learned in all those years in the Adventist church.

When I heard Lois Roden talk about the femininity of the Holy Spirit, it hit me like a ton of bricks. It made so much sense, I grasped it. I just took hold of that and I've never doubted it, just like I have never doubted the Sabbath day. I don't keep the Sabbath very well, but there are some truths that come to you. It's just all in the scriptures if you are looking for it. If you've never heard about it, it will just slip right over you.

David would come and visit me and get me so excited about the things he had learned. That's how I knew that God was working with David. I knew I hadn't been any help in his childhood and upbringing and with his learning disability. Now he was learning so much, I just knew God was leading him. I went and visited him quite a few times. I'd take my nephews, Patrick and Chris, with me.

David was staying with Lois Roden and working. Then for some reason he moved to Keene, Texas, where Southwestern Adventist University is located. I don't know if Lois told him he needed to go off on his own. I guess he was having some struggles or problems. I don't know.

David moved to Keene and was doing some construction on a big house there, working on a big three-story house for the Fryes, who were an Adventist family. He was staying in a duplex. Harriet and I went down there and spent the night with him. He had fasted for days and days. He used to fast a lot, because he was trying to learn. He looked terrible to me, skinny and malnourished. Eventually he went back to Mount Carmel.

I visited Mount Carmel just a few times, usually for one day. Once in a while I'd spend the night. David was always saying, "You gotta come for Passover, Mama." He wanted me to come to this and come to that.

David married Rachel Jones in 1984.[16] He brought Rachel to see me in Chandler the day they got married. They stopped here, and then they went over to Harriet's, and that's where they had their honeymoon.

David and the Core Group of Branch Davidians Leave Mount Carmel

I went to visit at Mount Carmel in 1983 and George Roden was up on the podium in the church with a gun strapped to his belt. That's when I heard the story that Vernon had raped his mother. I almost got up and left. It was not true.[17]

I guess the next time I saw the group they had all moved over to Herring Street in Waco. Rachel was pregnant. I had heard that David got run off from Mount Carmel and moved to Herring Street. Some of the people had already moved because George was causing a lot of problems. I went to visit. I remember seeing Clive. He was a little skinny guy and he was teaching the kids, since they were not being sent to public school.

I went there one day. When I arrived most of the people were gone, but Floyd Houtman's wife was there and also the Houtman children and Novellette Sinclair.[18] Everyone else was gone. They must have gone out somewhere. I was going to spend the night. Clive Doyle, his mother Edna Doyle, and Clive's two daughters, Karen and Shari, had a big front bedroom with four beds. Edna gave me her bed. She slept with one of the girls.[19]

David Bunds and his sister Robyn Bunds were staying there. I remember Robyn hugging me and saying, "You're so soft, like my mama." I fell in love with that little girl.[20]

Rachel and David were living out in the back of the house in a school bus that he had bought and fixed up. I went there two or three times. I took my nephews one time and spent the night.

In the meantime, David and Rachel went to Israel. She was pregnant. He wanted her to have the baby in Israel.[21] They had been over there a couple of months when they called me and said they were coming home, and asked me to meet them at the airport. Rachel was going to have that baby in a few weeks. So I went to the Dallas-Fort Worth International Airport and met them. They went home to Herring Street, and she had the baby in April and Passover was right after that.

I went to spend Passover with them in Mexia, Texas, just outside Waco. That's when they were leaving Waco and going to Mexia, and not all of them had moved to Mexia yet. There was a church campground there where someone let them stay. It was pretty run down. There was a big old house and another building and a church, all in ramshackle condition. I remember everyone was coming in. Rachel had just had that baby, Cyrus,[22] and they had put her back behind the kitchen or somewhere, and she didn't sleep very well. I was sleeping out in the car. It wasn't very comfortable, so on the next night I rented a motel room and put Rachel and the baby in there, and here comes Perry, Rachel's father, too!

I was there for two or three days and I got sick since it was allergy season. David was giving Bible studies, and I got a taste of his very first studies. I taped them. He was sort of awkward at that time. I met my grandson Cyrus. I looked at this funny little alien guy and I thought, "Oh, am I going to like this guy?" Novellette Sinclair was there, and Sheila Martin came from North Carolina for Passover.[23]

Then I returned home. I had to go back to work. The next thing I knew they called me and said they had moved on to Palestine, Texas. They were camping out among the trees, and had a little lean-to and that was about it. They were out in the middle of the woods.[24]

I think David paid $40,000 for the property at Palestine. It was twenty acres and it was $2,000 per acre, which was way too much because there was an electrical easement, with one of those big power lines, going down the side of it. It was mostly woods and there wasn't any water or electricity or anything. David bought it from a Mr. Milan. Mr. Milan called me after all of that happened in '93 and asked if I was going to keep the payments up. I didn't.

I'd go down to visit them at the Palestine camp. It was convenient for me, because it's so close to Chandler. It is only thirty-five miles from my house. They didn't have running water and they didn't have refrigerators and all that. One time I baked a bunch of sweet potato pies for them. One time I brought a bunch of watermelons. I'd take ice to them. It was just right up my alley to do things like that. By then I had made some friends among the group—Novellette and different ones.

The property was mostly pine trees. The payments were $400 a month. They moved there and set up a little lean-to shed for cooking, and I think they moved David's bus down there. They had to haul water in. I wish someone had kept up the payments after the fire.

I went down there to visit quite often. I would take jugs of frozen water, watermelons and different things, and come home at night.

BONNIE HALDEMAN BECOMES A BRANCH DAVIDIAN

Conflict with Roy

I was working for David Wilkerson at the time and I was frustrated over a lot of things. My husband was a heavy drinker. He was drinking more and more, and Roger had gotten in trouble at times. I was very unsatisfied with my life. Things were bad, so I'd go down to the Palestine camp and visit there.

During the summer of 1985, David, Perry Jones, Catherine Matteson, and a bunch of them went to the General Conference of the Seventh-day Adventist Church meeting in New Orleans,[25] so I invited Rachel to my house to stay for a few days. Cyrus was just a baby, my grandbaby. I didn't want her to come and live there or anything. I had them over and we went shopping. We looked in the Thrifty Nickel and I found a lady who had a baby bed for sale. We went and bought it, and brought it home and set it up in the living room. We went and bought a lot of things. David came back to Palestine from New Orleans to pick up something, so he stopped by our house on his motorcycle, and we weren't there.[26] I don't know what Roy said to David, but Roy said something like, "I ain't taking your family to raise." David went to Palestine to get the van, and he came back and loaded up Rachel, the baby, the baby bed and everything, and said, "Mama, I'll never be back." I didn't know what had happened. No one told me. I couldn't get it out of anyone. Roy was probably drinking. That was one of the things that led to my wanting to leave. Roy drank a lot then, and he just did and said a lot of things. I know I'm not perfect either, but I think God arranged it for me to leave.

I came home one night, and Roy and some other guys were all drunk out in the backyard. I pulled up and came in. I'd been planning on going to Palestine the next day any way. I had my stuff all packed so I could visit for the day. Roy was drunk, and when I came in I got mad. I went to bed in the spare bedroom. I was ticked off. I guess maybe I had been ticked off anyway. Roger was home and I asked Roger not to go off that night, but he did. Roy came in the house. He was drunk and I saw the devil in his eyes. Roy said something smart to me, and I just smarted back. I guess he was upset because I was in the spare bedroom. Three times he came in there and said terrible things to me. I just kept praying. It was a very upsetting night. Roger had gone off and I was there by myself.

The next morning Roy's truck was still there. He hadn't gone to work. "Ohhh, why didn't he go to work?" I decided I was going to go to Palestine to visit. I got some more stuff together, and I thought, "What should I do?" I snuck my stuff out and put it in the car. I didn't want to talk to Roy. I didn't know what to do. Then I heard this audible voice in my head say, "Go." It was the only time I ever heard something like that. I thought it was God who said, "Go." So I went and I didn't come back. I was so mad. I felt like I'd looked in the devil's eyes three times that night.

David and Rachel weren't in Palestine so I stayed in David's bus.[27] Every day I was gone it was easier. When David came back to the camp I went and bought a little tent and other supplies. I'd drive an hour and a half one-way to go to work at David Wilkerson's place.

When Roy sobered up he didn't know where I was. I came back to the house when I knew he was at work. I found out later that on the day they were drinking they had finished up a job and there was no need to go to work the next day. When I saw Roger at the house, he said, "Mama, where have you been? We've been worried." I told him, "I ain't coming back, Roger." He said, "Do what you gotta do, Mama." I said, "Just tell him I ain't coming back."

So I stayed at the Palestine camp. I went back and forth to work. Roy came down there one day. I said, "I ain't coming back." My Uncle Johnny used to live right up the street and he brought the preacher out to talk with me, but I wasn't there. It wasn't long afterwards that David, my mother, and I were taken off the church books and disfellowshipped.

I was very unhappy living with Roy at that time. I heard that voice in me and I went. I don't ever regret going, because if I hadn't left on August 12, 1985, I would never have known my grandkids or had those years with David or any of them. David didn't even know I was coming. David and Rachel and the baby were in California.

Life in the Palestine Camp

I settled in at the camp. I had friends there and they all welcomed me. At first I stayed in David's bus.

When I first started visiting there, they had a smaller camp up closer to the road, which was still in the middle of a bunch of trees. It was like a pine forest there. It was beautiful. They had a big lean-to for cooking and two or three buses to live in. David had a school bus, and I think a couple of others had school buses.

By the time I moved down there, they had cleared more of the property and made a road and relocated further back into the acreage. It was just a beautiful site. It had huge trees. By that time there were about five or six buses. They took all the seats out of the buses to make living quarters. The Doyles had one. David's bus was there. Perry and Mary Belle Jones had a bus, and they shared one end of it with Catherine Matteson. I think Wayne and Sheila Martin had a bus.[28] The buses just sort of fanned out from the camp in different directions.

To get to the camp you drove down an electrical easement, probably about the equivalent of half a block, and then turned onto the trail they had made about halfway in, at a huge pine tree we called the Trinity Tree, because it had three big trunks growing out of it. It was beautiful. It was so big, it had probably been there a hundred years. Then you'd go on a winding road into the camp.

The camp was pretty sparse with a little shed built out of roughhewn boards and timber boards and a little tin thing they had set up as the cook shack with a little storage place at the end. It was very crude.

At that time Clive's mother, Edna, was doing the cooking. Some of the girls would help. There were not a whole lot of people there at that time. None of the people from Hawaii and different places had come yet. I went to WalMart and bought a little 8' x 10' tent and different things I thought I needed for camping out—a lantern, flashlight, and I set it up in the back. The Kendricks were there in a tent. I think Brenda and Janet stayed in it mostly, so Bob must have been somewhere else. I think Bob, Janet's husband, was in Waco.[29]

It was a nice little thing. It was in the summertime and it was hot. We had no electricity, no fans, no refrigerators, no running water, but I was happy.

I had my car. The number of cars was limited. We would go into town to the convenience store and fill up our water jugs and buy things. We might buy ice to keep something cold.

At that time we were keeping the Daily twice a day at 9:00 in the morning and 3:00 in the afternoon. We'd stop what we were doing and have our Emblems, a little bit of grape juice and a small cracker. It's the Lord's Supper representing Christ's blood and his life that he shed for us. We'd have an hour of Bible study and we'd pray. We were real strict with that at that time. Edna usually made the bread.

We'd have our Bible studies out under the trees where the bus seats were arranged in a circle. That was where we'd have our meetings in the morning and the afternoon and then on Sabbath.

It was rustic, but it was fun. At night you would go wherever you could and wash up. You can take a pretty good bath with a gallon of water.

David came back from California after I'd been there about a week, and he didn't know I was there. He was glad to see me. They started building a main building for a kitchen and for the worship area. There was an old abandoned sawmill about a mile away at the road that turned off to come to the property. Floyd Houtman and Stan Sylvia[30] and some other guys got a bunch of the old roughhewn logs and cut them up to construct a building. It was probably forty to fifty feet long, and about twenty feet wide. The kitchen wasn't built yet. When they built it, David asked what did we want, a floor or a roof? Of course, we wanted a roof, so they put a roof on it. The building had just a couple of windows in it. Then they dug a root cellar in back of the building. Next they built a kitchen in the building with a wood floor. They framed it up and put a screen all around. It had a little storeroom. We stored potatoes and onions and other things in the summer cellar.

It was a lot of fun. I would drive back to the Tyler area to work in the evenings. I drove about sixty to sixty-five miles one way to get to work. I started work about 4:00 in the afternoon cleaning offices for David Wilkerson. If I had some new construction cleanup to do, I'd go work all day, but at that time, there wasn't much of that going on. That was later on. To clean the offices, I'd go in about 4:00 and work until about 10:00 or midnight. Some nights I would drive all the way back to Palestine, and get in about midnight or 1:00 in the morning. Some nights I would just camp out on the couch to sleep, and then get up early and leave. A few times I went to my mother's house and spent the night instead of driving all that way back. Her house was halfway between the job and Palestine.

I started taking some of the girls to work with me. Clive's daughters, Shari and Karen Doyle, and Novellette Sinclair went with me a lot. They all liked to go because we'd take showers. There were restrooms with showers in the bus barn where the medical office was. When you live out in the woods it is always a treat to have a nice shower. Some nights we'd just stretch out on the carpet and sleep and go back to Palestine in the morning. We did that three times a week—Sunday, Tuesday, and Thursday nights—and it went on from August until February.

Of course, Roy was upset with me. He wanted me to come home and I wouldn't do it. While he was at work I would sometimes go by the house and make ten or twelve sweet potato pies before I went to work. Slowly I was taking stuff that I needed from the house while he was gone. Sometimes he would be there and I'd talk to him, but usually I avoided him. Finally I guess he decided I wasn't going to come back home.

My daddy died in December of that year. We had the funeral over in Van, Texas and he was buried there at the cemetery. David was in California at that time, so he didn't get to come to the funeral.[31]

After the funeral I went back to Palestine. We didn't keep Christmas,[32] but I remember standing in line at WalMart thinking about my daddy and I started crying. I missed him. You always miss a parent, I guess, when they're gone.

By January it was cold! Some of the people didn't have any heat in their buses. I was lucky to have a small Dearborn heater that I took from the house. I got a round portable propane tank and hooked up the heater inside David's bus. I was still using David's bus, because David and Rachel were living in California. David would come to Palestine sometimes, but Rachel and Cyrus weren't living in the Palestine camp. A tank of gas didn't run very long, but I turned on the heater only at night when I was going to wash up, change clothes, or in the mornings to take the chill off. Clive's daughters started coming in and staying with me a lot, because I had heat. Their grandmother, Edna, didn't have heat. That little ol' woman could stand anything.

We had a big wood stove in the main building and people would go in there to get warm. We had kerosene lanterns and flashlights. We didn't have any electricity. A telephone line was run all the way out to the road through the woods. The telephone was in the little shed close to the building, so we did have communications.

David would come back and give Bible studies and get things going to improve the camp.

Some of the men at the camp at that time were doing roofing in Waco: Clive Doyle, Wayne Martin, David Bunds, and some others. They went off and did roofing during the week, slept in their cars, and came home on the weekend. So it was mostly women and kids around the camp most of the time during the week. We'd go to town and do our laundry at the washateria.

Perry Jones was doing the shopping. Not many people had cars. I had a car. Janet Kendrick had a car. I don't know if Perry had a car or not. He'd just use whatever car was around. Perry was the one who was in charge of the camp when David was gone, so whatever he said went. We didn't buy a lot of groceries at one time, because we didn't have refrigeration. Perry would go into town to shop. I remember we'd still be waiting at 7:00 p.m. for him to get back so we could have something for supper. He'd get hung up in town doing I don't know what.

David took Edna out of the kitchen and started having the younger women, like Novellette Sinclair and Janet Kendrick and others, cook. Edna loved doing it, but maybe she loved it too much. I don't know.

Catherine Matteson was never allowed to help in the kitchen. At that time Catherine was going through a hard time with her eyes, and I think she was probably legally blind. At times she was taken to Dallas to see an eye doctor. She used to buy 50-pound bags of carrots and blend them up to make carrot juice. It was supposed to help her eyes. Evidently it worked. Something did. Over the years her sight got better.

Adventures in California

In February of '86 David called and said I could come out to California. Four of us went. I had a little 1980 Oldsmobile. It was a good little car. David told Catherine Matteson, Joel Jones, Brother Lawter, and me to come out to California to the house in San Bernadino. Joel Jones is a son of Perry and Mary Belle Jones. He's Rachel's brother. Brother James Lawter was blind in one eye and couldn't see out the other. He's passed on since then. He came out of Mount Carmel during the siege and went to jail.[33] He was really nice. He called me Sister Bonnie.

I drove us out to California. Catherine didn't drive, of course, and Joel didn't drive, and Brother Lawter wanted to help me drive. He'd say, "Sister Bonnie, won't you let me drive?" "Oh no, Brother Lawter, I'm doing fine." I was afraid to let him drive!

We had a nice trip. We stopped two or three times along the way. I think we stopped one night in a motel in El Paso. The four of us shared a room for half a night. We got up early and left.

This was a new adventure for me, because I'd never been to California. I was looking forward to it, because Rachel was out there with my grandson, Cyrus. That was February, and Cyrus was going to be one in April. I hadn't been able to spend much time with him, so I was really tickled to go to California.

I took a vacation from work. I still worked for the Wilkersons. I wasn't self-employed. They paid me a salary, so I took a two-week vacation. I called later and told them I wasn't coming back.

When we got to California, David had already left, which disappointed me greatly. David and Clive had gone to Australia, and he had left the day before, I think.[34]

Rachel and Cyrus were there. Jimmy Riddle was already there. As a matter of fact, when we arrived, we were driving up Fifth Street, and saw Jimmy walking up the street. I didn't recognize him. He had long hair.[35] When we got to the house, they were all gone except for Rachel, who was really glad to see us. I think the main reason David had me come to California was to be with Rachel and Cyrus, because he was going to be gone for a while in Australia.

The house was on Fifth Street in San Bernadino. Actually it wasn't far from downtown San Bernadino. If you turned left off of I-10, you went into Loma Linda. If you turned right you'd go into San Bernadino. You didn't go very far before you turned right on Fifth Street. It was just down about a mile. It wasn't too far from the Air Force base. Fifth Street was a busy street. The house was a little ol' stucco with three bedrooms, one bath, a small kitchen, a fair-sized living room, and a small dining room. I don't think there was any grass in the yard. I think there was a guy living in the back in a truck topper. I don't know where he came from. He came with the house. His name was Frank, and he always said he was miserable.

We rented this house from a lady named Rosie. She had a bunch of rental property. Another woman, Gail, had grown up in the house. Gail's family had lived there for a long time. She was a drug user and she left all her stuff there, but she never paid rent. I guess David agreed to let Gail stay there and leave her stuff there. She was in and out, in and out. She got to be a friend, but it was just a weird, weird situation. She was something else. We would feed her and try to help her.

That's the way David was. He was kind. Even though we were paying the rent and had moved in, he let her stay there. As more of us came we needed room. Catherine and I took the room in the back. Jimmy and Clive were already staying there; they may have camped out in the living room. David and Rachel had their bedroom.

It was about the middle of February, so it was still pretty chilly at night. The days were nice, but I remember it snowed when we were there. You could look out and see snow on the San Bernadino mountains. Catherine knew some people in Redlands, so she and I went to visit them. I think they were old Davidians.

Perry Jones and David met Marc Breault in Loma Linda. Perry took me to the grocery store in Loma Linda so I could take over buying the groceries, handling the money, and cooking. When Perry and I were in Loma Linda I met Marc Breault for the first time at the grocery store. He was going to the Adventist College there. Marc Breault lived there in an apartment, and he was studying to be a minister. When he graduated, they wouldn't let him be a minister, I guess because he was blind.[36]

Marc Breault, as everyone knows, joined with us. He eventually married Elizabeth Baranyai from Australia, and they were the ones who started this stuff about child abuse and everything against David before the ATF raid on Mount Carmel, but that was a lot later down the road.

As I was saying, there were just a few of us at the house in San Bernadino. I took over running the house and was enjoying my grandson. I was introduced to a couple of ladies that David had met. They both had nursing homes in their homes—bed and board for elderly people. I felt like I needed to work. One lady let me start coming to clean. I cleaned the nursing home, which was in her home. The other lady had me come also. She was a prominent Adventist and she had a much nicer home. Her husband lived somewhere else. She'd go visit him on some weekends, so she'd have me come and stay while she was gone. I'd clean the house and help some of the ladies with their baths and cook meals. I did that while she was there, too, a couple days a week. When she wanted to go off for the weekend, I'd come stay with the ladies. It was a nice experience. It gave me a little money. That was in Redlands.

I stayed busy. I was driving around and getting to know California and enjoying what I saw. David came back and he took me to Don and Jeannine Bunds' house in the Glenwood area of Los Angeles. Over the years I had heard about their $150,000 home. She was a nurse and he was an engineer, and I thought, "Wow, they must have a beautiful place." I was so shocked when we went into the neighborhood. The homes were old. It was a nice little house, but it was probably built in the '40s. It had three bedrooms with the master bedroom upstairs. It had a pool in the back. That swimming pool was all the backyard could hold. It wasn't all that nice just because it was expensive. Here in Texas at that time a $150,000 house was NICE.

At one time they had a lot of people living there: David and Rachel, Clive, and others. They had quite a house full. The Bunds were big supporters of the Branch Davidians. Eventually they moved out to Waco.

We used to go into the churches around there, hand out literature, and meet people. Usually someone would invite us to their home for lunch after church. I always hated to hand out literature, but that was part of it. Sometimes people would take it, and sometimes they wouldn't. We met quite a few people who wanted to hear more, and David would bring them home, or we'd go to their homes.

It was a different experience for me. I loved driving around and being there, because it was the first time I'd ever been in California. When we were kids my mother had always talked about going to California some day. She never made it there.

David came back to California and then went to Palestine. That's about the time Rachel started staying in her room a lot. She was down in the dumps. She wasn't feeling good. David wasn't there, and he called and had us studying the charts that Brother Houteff had made. I remember he called one night and Rachel was talking to him, and he told Rachel the Lord had told him to take another wife. This was in March or early April 1986. Rachel had been moping around and we didn't know she was pregnant at the time. She told David that she had a dream, and she knew that the Lord had told him to take another wife. It bothered her. That's why she was staying to herself. She told him, "I know." I know she was upset about it, but she said, "I know, because the Lord told me in a dream that He was going to tell you that."[37]

So that's what I had to go by. He had been struggling with that, too. He told everyone out at Palestine, which included Novellette and Wayne Martin, and it really upset them. Novellette said, "Is my Bible deceiving me?" It really upset them. It was a blow to the situation. And he told them who the new wife was going to be. He had us studying those charts and this particular person sort of looked like a person on the chart. That's one thing David did. David didn't just tell us, "This is what this means." He had us study it first. He had us study a lot of things so we could come up with the answer ourselves before he told us what it was.

That's how I remember that happening. I guess Rachel accepted it. She didn't say anything to us. Rachel was very close-mouthed. In the meantime, we found out that she was pregnant, too. She was pregnant with Star. Cyrus was turning a year old.[38]

There was a lot of upset and questions in the Palestine camp. It was just a handful of us out there in California. It was blow to all of us. I think it tested the faith of a lot of people, especially some of the older ones like Novellette and Wayne Martin. This wife never had any children. She was supposed to and she was really excited. She was very young, fourteen. And she accepted it.[39]

April was Passover time. David wanted everyone in California to go back to Texas for Passover. They bought a bus, and David drove us back to Texas. Clive stayed at the house in San Bernadino. Just after we left, Ofelia Santoyo, Jean Borst and her son Brad, came to the house in a little car. Clive told them how to get to Palestine.[40]

We were in Palestine for Passover week. Sheila Martin was pregnant with Daniel and she wanted to go to California to have the baby. I rode back to California with Sheila and Wayne and we stopped in El Paso to see Wayne's brother in the middle of the night, but he wasn't there. We went on back to San Bernadino and opened up the house, and then Sheila decided she didn't want to have the baby there so they left and drove to the northeast. A couple of days later David came back with a bunch of people in the bus. He sent me over to Rosie's to stay, because she needed someone to housesit. Rosie was our landlady.

I went to work. I went over to Rosie's and stayed and I was working for the other two ladies with the nursing homes. As time went on, I got some houses to clean. I think Clive helped me on a couple of them. I also visited different churches with the group on Sabbath and handed out literature. David would come and go, back and forth from Palestine at different times.

I think it was through Marc Breault and some of his friends from Hawaii that David went to Hawaii, and started giving studies to people like Margarida and Neil Vaega, Paul Fatta, Judy and Steve Schneider, Peter Hipsman, Sherri Jewell, and Cita [Floracita] and Scott Sonobe.[41] He met that group of people through Marc Breault, and he gave them Bible studies. One day when David was back in California, he said to me, "Come on. We're going to the park. We're going to meet Paul Fatta, and Sherri Jewell's coming over." They were in California for something. So that was the first time I met them. I thought Sherri Jewell was the most beautiful woman I ever saw.

During this time, we had an arrangement with a fruit stand in Redlands. It was a big one. California has really nice fruit stands. We would go there twice a week and everything that they culled out we could have. That was a lot of what we would eat on our very limited budget. Me being a country girl, we started canning. I went around to all the thrift stores and bought all the canning jars I could find. One of the ladies I was working for, who boarded elderly people needing care in her home, loaned me a big water bather and she gave me a bunch of jars, because she did canning, too. I was busy and I enjoyed it. We canned plums and peaches. We didn't can anything that required a pressure cooker because I didn't have one. We canned tomatoes, and all kinds of fruits. We ate all that stuff and we had a lot of popcorn.

We had Bible studies. I remember it being hot in California, but it was enjoyable. I had been tied down for years and years with a husband. It was a whole different experience for me. I'd take my grandson, Cyrus, shopping with me and I just enjoyed that. I was there when Cyrus started walking. I was having a good time.

Then David and Steve Schneider came over and we met him. I think Steve had a cousin who was there. David decided to send Jimmy Riddle and me back to Palestine, and this young man, Steve's cousin, needed a ride to Palestine or somewhere. Clive was going to go, too. We packed beaucoodles of canned vegetables into Clive's old truck and were ready to go late at night when it was decided that we'd leave in the morning. By the next morning, David changed his mind and kept Clive in California so it was Jimmy and me in the old truck with no air conditioning. Jimmy was my traveling buddy. We let the cousin drive at some point, and the pedal fell off a motorcycle that was ahead of us. It bounced on the road and went straight through our windshield.

I remember we got somewhere on this side of Arizona and ran out of gas. We coasted off the highway. We got off on a feeder road and started up this hill, and we got barely to the top of the hill where the overpass was, came to a stop sign, and the truck just stopped—no gas. So we looked, and there's nothing out there. We're looking down this little side road that crosses the freeway and we saw a sign for a convenience store up the little country road. The three of us got the truck out of gear and started pushing it. We pushed that truck all the way up there and got gas. I guess we were lucky. God was looking out for us that we were able to get gas. We had that truck loaded with all kinds of canned goods, cases and cases of stuff we had canned.

I don't remember what happened to that boy. I guess we dropped him off at the airport or Perry took him. He flew back to Wisconsin.

Everyone was so happy to see all that food. I was horrified, because with the amount of people that we had, they'd open twenty jars at a time. In no time at all it was gone.

Back in Texas

It was a good time. I was in California about six months. I had gone out there in April. It was getting to be fall when I got back to the Palestine camp. I moved into David and Rachel's bus, and I had a little heater set up in there.

I got my job back with David Wilkerson. One day I went to work and I came home and drove in and this little blond girl was standing there. Of course I knew Shari, Clive's daughter. She said, "I missed you. I wish you were my mama." Her mama had hardly raised her, because Clive got her back when she was about two. Clive and his mother, Edna, raised her. Shari just took to me, and my heart melted, so she started staying with me a lot, and then her sister, Karen, would come. They spent a lot of time with me. They'd go to work with me. That made some of the other girls jealous. I tried to take the different girls at different times. I took Anita Martin and Michele Jones. But Shari was the one I took all the time, and Karen. They would stay with me.[42]

Although it was fall it was hot. We would have the meetings and go lay out in the back of the buses with the doors open to try to stay cool. We still didn't have any electricity. Novellette was glad to have me back. It was at that time that they said Rachel was coming back. David was sending Rachel back. She was pregnant with Star. So I got word that I had to move out of the bus.

I wanted my own bus. I got to calling and looking around. I found out through someone that they were having an auction at Wills Point Public School. I gave them a bid on a bus, and since we were a church group, I got it. It was a big school bus. A lot of people had them. David and Rachel had one, and the Martins and the Doyles had theirs. The Doyles' bus was painted white. It was an old one and smaller. Perry had one that was all broke down, but we eventually used it as a school room for the kids.

I don't remember how we got to Wills Point. I remember Stan Sylvia drove the bus back to Palestine with Clive and me sitting in the back seats. I got the bus and had it parked where I wanted it. I didn't live in it until after I came back from Hawaii. There were different people coming by then, people from Australia, several families, and different ones coming out and building little plywood huts.

I went back to California, and then David decided to send me to Hawaii. He sent Jimmy and me to Hawaii in March of '87.

Hawaii

David had already been over to Hawaii and met all our people there. Margarida and Neil Vaega had a bakery in Hawaii. David wanted them to come eventually to California and open up a restaurant there. He sent Jimmy and me on an airplane to Hawaii and that's the first time I met Neil and Margarida and Peter Hipsman, Greg Summers,[43] Judy and Steve Schneider, and Scott and Cita Sonobe. The Vaegas had a fourplex behind the bakery, and they were all living in it. There were two apartments upstairs. Judy and Steve had one apartment with Greg Summers and Peter, and Margarida and Neil had one. Jimmy moved in with Steve and Judy, and I moved in with the Vaegas. Neil's sister, Ness, was staying there, too.

David sent Jimmy and me over there to learn how to run the bakery, because Neil and Margarida had given the bakery to the church. He wanted me to learn how to run it, so Margarida and Neil could come over to California and open a bakery and restaurant there. Ness Vaega was there and she thought she was going to run the bakery. They put me to work but as time went on they weren't giving me any authority. Neil and Margarida and Ness would do the banking and the ordering and buying, and I was left there to do the baking, but they didn't even teach me to bake. I heard Ness talking on the phone to a friend one day, saying, "I'm going to run this bakery when they go to California." I told her one day, "You know, I was sent here to learn to run this thing." They all got mad at me. I think I said something to David. I felt bad, but I wasn't learning what I was supposed to because of Ness taking over. Then after a few months, David sent Clive over there. When Neil and Margarida went over to the States from Hawaii they let their other daughter, Ursula, run it, but it folded up. David sent Clive and Scott Sonobe out for a while, too, with Margarida. Margarida sold it in December.

In September, after six months, we all packed up, every one of us. We were just going to leave it. I remember packing up a bunch of stuff out of the kitchen to have it shipped back. They were selling furniture and everything. Margarida sold all kinds of stuff. We had a garage sale. We went to Palestine: the Schneiders, Greg Summers, Peter Hipsman, all of us, and we just left everything else sitting that we didn't sell. Actually we all went to California first. We were all crowded into that house.

I remember riding back on the plane. A storm came and we didn't get the plane that we wanted, and it was late at night. The storm was just pounding our plane, and it was jumping up and down. It was very scary.

Back in California

When we got back in San Bernadino we started baking. Margarida started baking bagels and making sandwiches with whole wheat bread. Jimmy and different ones would go out to office buildings and sell sandwiches and bagels with cream cheese at lunchtime. It was a nice little business, but for the number of people who were working it wasn't turning any profit to speak of, even though we didn't get paid.

When I came back on the plane from Hawaii, Michele Jones was at the house. Michele and Sherri Jewell were there with her little girl, Kiri. I don't remember if Rachel was there or not. There wasn't anyone in the front bedroom but me, and I knew Michele was sleeping back in the music room. I told her to come up to the front bedroom and sleep with me, but she didn't like it. She wouldn't do it. She said something to David, and David jumped all over me. I got to putting two and two together. I didn't know it at that time, but I guess Michele was already one of his wives.[44] Sherri Jewell was, too, I guess.

There was a guy there, Andre, who came from Hawaii with us. He had been a homosexual but gave it up. He went back to Palestine with us. He had AIDS and eventually he died after we moved back to Waco.

Return to Palestine

Eventually a whole bunch of us ended up in the Palestine camp. We all came back together in the bus. Scott Sonobe had a little house at the camp. Paul Fatta had built a little house. We had a whole lot of square little houses out in the woods. Ruth Ottman [later Riddle] and her mother, Gladys Ottman, had a house.

It seemed like the majority of us were there at Palestine for a while. That's when Novellette began living in the front of my bus. The Gents had been living in the back of my bus while I was away. They were building a little house. The Gents were the parents of Peter, the young man shot on the watertower during the ATF raid on February 28, 1993 and Nicole, who in 1993 was pregnant with a baby and had Dayland, a little boy, and Paige, a little girl.[45] When I got back to Palestine I guess the Gents were in the process of moving into the little house they had built.

Novellette had stored all my stuff in her end of the bus. She took real good care of it. My bus was still up in the front of the camp, in the middle. David told us all to start deciding where we wanted the buses lined up. I put my bus at the very end where you came off the easement onto the road so we would have more privacy. We had it dragged and pushed to that location. My bus was the first one you passed coming into the camp. Then came Edna and Clive's bus, and then Larry and Stan's bus. Novellette and I went and bought a wood stove. Clive installed it for us. I went to my mother's house and got my antique iron bed and brought it up there. It was my bus, so I got the back end. I had a chest of drawers from home, which my grandmother had given me. I had my bed, that chest of drawers, and my pot at the end of my bed. Then came the wood stove, then Novellette's bed, and a cabinet for her clothes. We took the seat out of the front end so there was storage space, and room for Snuggles, my little dog.

Snuggles was a Lhasa Apso. I found Snuggles on one of my trips from the fruit market at Redlands. I was coming home with a load and had just pulled up to make a left turn into our driveway, and here's this little puppy out in the middle lane of the road. Clive was in the front yard. I stopped. I couldn't turn. The puppy was lying there, and I think Clive saw him about the same time I did. I hollered, "Come get this puppy!" So he got the puppy and we claimed joint ownership. I think Clive named him Snuggles. He sat outside and held and held that puppy. David wouldn't let us bring him into the house. Snuggles would cry and cry, and we'd hold him.

We took Snuggles to the vet. We went around the neighborhood to see if he belonged to anyone. The vet said he was six months old. We got his shots and took him to Palestine with us. I left Snuggles there in the care of Novellette and Edna when I went to Hawaii. They were taking care of him, and I supported him. I remember Edna said one time that he got so matted they had to hold him down and cut all his hair off. He loved the road. As a matter of fact, that's what finally got him, that road in front of my house in Chandler. That's why I put that $700 fence up. He never did stay in it. I had him about ten or eleven years, and he got out there in the road in front of my house in Chandler.

Novellette decided Snuggles couldn't come to the back of the bus. The front door was as far as he could go. I was a little offended. It was my bus! I think Snuggles knew that. Every time she'd go out, he'd come in and get right in the middle of her bed. He was a cute little thing. Anyway Edna and Novellette helped take care of him. He was as at home in Clive and Edna's bus as he was in mine.

When I started moving in my bus we built a place to shower around the front of the bus made with black plastic. We'd use it when the weather was nice. We stacked some wood there, and that's where we'd do our showers. In the summertime you can make a good shower with a gallon or two of water. In the winter you more or less had to wipe up. We'd empty our buckets in the sand out in the woods. I had gotten my job back, so we would shower at work and sometimes go to my mom's house for a shower. Novellette went to work with me a lot. That little ol' wood stove would heat that bus up. It'd get sort of warm when it was hot. It would really heat up nice.

I enjoyed my time there. I remember one night it was 2:00 in the morning and someone came pounding at the door. It was Sherri Jewell. Then David came in a little bit later. It was Mother's Day and he had recorded a song about mothers: there ought to be a hall of fame for mothers. I've still got it. He sent me a little book about mother. It was sweet. When I was in Hawaii working, he called me on Mother's Day and sang "Happy Mother's Day" over the phone.

That last time I came back from California, Clive, Karen, someone else and I had started out to come to Texas and my car broke down. We ended up having the car towed back to San Bernadino. I had to leave my car there and rode back to Palestine with Jimmy Riddle.

When I got to Palestine I was stuck without a car. Janet Kendrick let me use her car. I drove her car to World Challenge for a while—they let me come back and do some cleaning. Paul Fatta bought a van and gave it to the association. Different people had driven it, but he said I could drive it. I didn't have my job at David Wilkerson's any more, so I went back into the house cleaning business. I got some jobs in Dallas. So Novellette and I were cleaning new houses in Dallas where we stayed with some people and were working out of that van. We'd go home on the weekends. We did BIG houses. We made some money.

So many things happened, if you think of one thing, you think about something else. It was a busy time. We had a lot of people coming there. It was a lot of people and we had a lot to do to live there. We had to haul water, go to town and do laundry, and different things.

The Community Organization

I've called the group an "association" and I've called it a "church." We were Branch Davidians. The official name from Ben Roden's time was General Association of Branch Davidian Seventh-day Adventists, BDSDA for short.[46] Under Lois it was still the same thing, but she tacked on Living Waters Branch. In fact, for a little while, just a very short while, David called it Davidian Branch Davidians. He said it twice to show the Davidian message was being revitalized.

However, the people who were joining did not feel like they were joining the Branch Davidian church or the Branch Davidians. They were just studying the Bible.[47] It was kind of non-denominational in a sense. That is usually what we'd tell people when we'd talk to them.

When we started out, David focused his message on the Branch Davidians, but then it expanded to include Seventh-day Adventists. After awhile he started talking to everyone—on the street, in music stores. As people from different faiths came in, they were not joining Branch Davidians per se, they were students studying the scriptures. That name got dropped as far as referring to the group. It was still there on paper.[48]

The older members considered themselves former Branch Davidians or continuing Branch Davidians.

I am getting ahead of myself because the shootout with George Roden happened before Novellette and I started going to Dallas to work.

DAVID KORESH'S SHOOTOUT WITH GEORGE RODEN AT MOUNT CARMEL

In November 1987 George Roden dug up a lady's body out of the cemetery at Mount Carmel.[49] Anna Hughes had been dead for twenty years. George sent a challenge somehow to David that whichever one of them could resurrect this lady should be accepted as the next prophet. When David heard about it he said, "We are not here for that kind of stuff," and ignored him. David went down to the sheriff's office along with about eight of our guys and reported that George had dug up the body. They said they weren't going to do anything about it. They needed some proof first.[50]

So David and some of our guys drove down to Mount Carmel. David sent someone onto the Mount Carmel property and he took pictures of the coffin in the church. George had it in the front of the church with an Israeli flag draped over it. David and the guys took the pictures to the sheriff's department and said here's what we were talking about. And they said, yep, it sure looks like a coffin. It looks like it's been buried. It's all dirty and rusty. But how do we know whether there's anything in it? It could be empty. They said they needed more proof. As they were leaving someone in the sheriff's department said, you know that George Roden's crazy. He's got guns. You need to get yourself something to protect yourself with. That was the first time David went out and bought some guns.

David took eight guys in the van to drive to Mount Carmel. They all hauled out in the middle of the night. Perry drove and dropped them off at Mount Carmel. They went through the gate and laid in the ditch perusing the place. George was out there with big mastiff-type dogs. The guys laid out there watching. The dogs were barking. George looked around, and he didn't see anything because they are all laying in the ditch. One of them snuck into the church while the rest of them laid out keeping watch just in case the other person got caught. He went into the church and was supposed to get pictures inside the coffin. Apparently this individual came back and said that the coffin was not there anymore, it had been moved. Now what are we going to do? David told them, we are going to circle all the way around to the back. Don't go off the property. They went out to the barn (the dairy) at the back end of the property and they stayed there the rest of the night.

In the morning David said, we are going to go from house to house, building to building, and see if we can find out what he's done with the coffin. George had some church members living back there in some of the houses. A lot of the houses were abandoned, but two or three of them had people in them, so when they came to a house, they knocked. If it was abandoned or empty they opened the door. When they came to one and found that someone was there, they spoke to them. I don't know how they explained why they were there, but they said it might be a good idea if you either stay indoors or leave the property. We don't want any trouble. They didn't have any trouble until one person went scurrying down and told George that there were men on the property and that some of them had guns. George was living in his mother's house at the time. Lois Roden had died in '86. This was in November or December 1987.

So the guys were going down to the front of the property hiding behind things as they went. When they got down towards George's end of the property they ran into problems when George came out. I guess Floyd Houtman and Stan Sylvia were out in front with everyone else trailing behind. Floyd and Stan were caught flat-footed out in the open and George started shooting at them. The Administration Building had burned down in spring 1983 and all that was left was the foundation. So these two big guys from Boston hit the ground and tried to hide behind the concrete foundation while George shot at them. David kind of peeked around the corner to see what was happening and said, damn, they're about to get killed. He said that he grabbed his gun and ran out into the field. He ran behind an abandoned car and he started shooting up in the air but in George's direction over his head. George panicked and ran behind a skinny tree, which looked kind of funny because George was so big he was showing on both sides of the tree. David said that he started shooting the tree, peppering the wood, to keep George locked in there so he wouldn't shoot at Stan and Floyd. Apparently one of David's bullets ricocheted because it hit the magazine of George's gun and jammed it and hit George's hand. So the story went out that David had gone out there to kill George, when he had gone out there to take pictures for the sheriff's department. Amo Roden, whatever her name was at the time, called the cops.[51] The sheriff came out and the guys surrendered and laid down on the ground. They are all arrested and taken to jail. David and Paul Fatta were bailed out, but the rest of them stayed in jail.[52]

When we came back from Hawaii I had a certain amount of money from the bakery. David said, "Just put it in the bank. It will be divided up." After the shootout, David called me and said, "Mama, get that money and bail me out." He could not stand jail. It scared him and so he was one of the first ones who got out. David told me, "Mama, I just can't take much of the jail." He had a fear of being locked up. Only David and Paul Fatta were bailed out. Later David Jones got bailed out.[53]

After the guys had been arrested and David got out of jail, David had some of us women standing guard at different times out at the entrance to the camp at Palestine keeping watch at the road. The women would stand guard with shotguns all around the clock watching the road, because they thought that maybe George would be coming down there. I remember that several nights I was out by the road on the right side of the property on the east side and I'd take Snuggles with me and Sheila's big ol' dog would go with me. Some nights I would hear coyotes and wolves. We would have four-hour shifts. It was scary in the middle of the night out there in those trees, but we had to watch the road because most of our guys were gone. It was an experience. Little kids were told to stay away as we would walk the campground. There wasn't but one way someone could get in and that was at the front, but we were quite a ways back in the woods. I still have the small gun David loaned me at that time.[54]

After the shootout and before the trial, George got himself arrested for writing letters to the judge, the sheriff's department and different lawyers cussing them out, telling them he was putting curses on them, they were going to get AIDS and herpes and all kinds of stuff, because he thought that they were not in his favor. He went to jail. While he was in jail, from my understanding, he did something and got his term extended, so he was in jail about a year.[55] So George was in jail, our guys were in jail, except David and Paul, and we got a call down at Palestine from David. He said, George is in jail, there are no church members on the property, it's time to reclaim our property.[56]

RESETTLING AT MOUNT CARMEL

David's Group Returns

Just about everyone at the Palestine camp rode back to Mount Carmel in the bus.[57] Perry had called the press so the reporters were all waiting at the gate when they drove up. The bus stopped outside the gate and they walked in. The story goes that Amo grabbed a gun and was going to come out and start shooting at them. Some other guy wrestled it off of her and said, don't be a fool, the press are here, they've got cameras. Amo came out when they were walking down the driveway, and Perry or someone said, David says that you who are living here are welcome to stay here if you choose, but you will not be paying rent to George anymore. So Amo was kind of in a huff. She got herself a knapsack, put some things in it, and left. The other people stayed for a while but eventually they all chose to leave rather than live with us. So by the time the trial came in '88, we were back in possession of the property.

The Trial for the Shootout

Mr. Coker was David's lawyer[58] and when the trial started Mr. Coker was allowing certain people to go in, but he wouldn't let me go in. But someone said, "That's his mother," so I got to go in eventually but I couldn't hear anything.[59]

When they moved back to Mount Carmel they found Anna Hughes' coffin.[60] It was stuck in a shed. During the trial they took the coffin to the courthouse. The judge wouldn't let it in the courtroom, but they got it up the stairs just outside his court. Anna wasn't in the coffin. She had been buried again.

The press came out to Mount Carmel for the burial. They kind of wrote it up like, they just dug a hole and stuck her in with no big ceremony or anything. She had already had a funeral. They were just putting her back where she belonged. Actually, they didn't put her in the same hole, they dug a fresh grave for her. But the reporters figured they should have had some big service for her.

Bonnie Moves to Mount Carmel

Novellette and I were working in Dallas[61] when they got the word after George had been arrested to come back and possess the land. We were sort of living out of the van, or with my friend. Novellette and I had already gone down to the trial and we went back to the Dallas area to finish up cleaning a house. We were working on a million dollar house over on the west side of Plano. We got it finished and we called someone, and they told us not to go back to Palestine, but to go to Mount Carmel.

Novellette and I got to Mount Carmel some time after they had returned. We went in and the place was just a pigsty. George had people living there who weren't even church members—dope dealers and all kinds of people. Everything was in disarray and trashed. The houses weren't painted and some of them were just dilapidated anyway. Doors were hanging off the hinges. The water ran in some houses, a little bit. Goats were running in and out of the buildings. It was a total mess.

Some of the people, like Clive and Edna, had moved back into the same houses they had lived in before. Other people moved in wherever they could or David assigned them homes. Novellette and I got back and of course we didn't have a house. There was one house that no one had taken. I think Rachel had tried to move in this one but it was full of stuff. It was actually one of the better houses there but he wouldn't let Rachel or anyone else move in there. It had boxes and boxes and boxes of stuff, just a lot of junk mail and clothes and other things. When we got there and didn't have a place to go, David said, "Ya'll take that house, but don't touch any of that stuff." We moved in and it was nasty with roach and rat droppings. We had to go back to Palestine and get our things, but we put a mattress in the bedroom. We cleaned it out so we would have a place to sleep temporarily while we cleaned it up. We cleaned and stacked all those boxes of junk in the living room and covered them with plastic. The boxes were full of old junk mail and sales papers, pots and pans, and other things. I found a few important things in there that I gave to David. As time went on, I just cleaned the house and got rid of that stuff.

David would not let anyone move into the little house in the back of the property. He told everyone to stay out of it. It was nasty.[62] David found books and recipes and paraphernalia in that house for cooking up methamphetamine. The house also had a lot of pornography in it. A couple had lived there who were doing mail-order pornography. David got rid of the pornography, and he took all of the drug paraphernalia down to the sheriff's office and just handed it to them. He should have gotten a receipt. I guess that's how the ATF agents came up with this accusation that we had a drug lab. But the drug lab was operated by these ex-convicts that George had living out there.[63]

I quit working in Dallas and Novellette was put in charge of the cooking at Mount Carmel.[64] At that time we were using the houses to cook in, but eventually they built a kitchen. We all got busy and painted the houses and they had to roof a lot of them. I remember Neil and Margarida Vaega built screens for my windows. Several people brought their little huts from Palestine. Margarida and Neil, and Steve and Judy did and they put them back in the back. The only bus that was brought from Palestine was Stan's. That's the one that was buried later to make a passageway between the large building and the storm shelter they were constructing.

I painted my house white with an aqua-colored trim. We had hardwood floors and I sanded them and put a fresh coat of polyurethane on them. It was the prettiest house there. Some of the houses had septic tanks and running water for a little while, then they got to where they wouldn't work. But we could stand in the bathtub and take our showers and save the water to flush the commode with.

So we moved back to Mount Carmel in '88. I got a little job in town and eventually David put me in charge of buying food and other things. They built the kitchen and dining area on the site of the Administration Building that had burned down. David built these so we would have a kitchen because it was getting really crowded trying to cook in one of the little houses. I guess it was the house Rachel was living in. The guys pitched in and built it. It was a pretty nice building. We had a lot of kitchen equipment that they had bought from a restaurant out in California.

That building got bigger and bigger. They built the kitchen and dining room area, then the chapel next to it and then as you went up the back stairs, David had two big rooms up there. They were built while I was there.

The Haldeman Family Reunites

Novellette and I lived in that little house. Roger came to Mount Carmel to live. He was living in a little brick house that I guess used to be a shower house. He lived out there behind my house for a while. Then Roy started coming up. I think that was in 1989. He brought the travel trailer. I wasn't living with him and I hadn't lived with him for several years. He pulled the trailer up right there beside the house. He stayed out there, and Novellette and I were living in the house. Roy wanted his family back.

Finally David said, "Mama, you may be the only means of Daddy's salvation. You know he never had any interest in religion." David said, "I'm not telling you what to do. It's up to you whether you want to take him back or not." Roy and I were still married. I had to have Novellette move out so Roy could move in. The grandkids loved that. Cyrus loved his grandpa. I don't know if it was because David was gone so much, but Cyrus loved Grandpa. Cyrus spent a lot of time with us. I got jealous because Cyrus and I had spent so much time together. Roy came into the picture and Cyrus just shifted mainly from me to him. Novellette moved into the house Roger had been in. Actually, it was pretty nice. It was all cement with a cement floor, and it even had a shower stall. Roger started staying in the travel trailer.

Roy moved in and we got some furniture and things that had been stored at Mama's home and made a nice little house. It was really nice. Roy was happy and when we went to the meetings, he would be the first one to jump up when the bell rang.

We had our regular meetings at 9:00 a.m., 3:00, p.m. and 7:00 p.m., but a lot of times at 10:00 or 11:00 at night David decided that he had to have a Bible study about something and would start ringing the bell. That bell would start ringing and everyone would get up and go. Roy always got up and was ready to go. He listened and maybe that was his salvation.

Roy had been living in Chandler while I was gone. Roger was with him and Roy took care of his brother, who had had a stroke, at our house for about a year and a half. Roy had been drinking a lot and was overweight. I think if he hadn't come down to Mount Carmel Roy would have been dead a lot earlier. He started eating right, quit drinking, and lost weight, but he'd sneak off every once in a while to have a few.

Nursing School

I started nursing school. First I studied to be a nurse's aid. A lady I was keeping house for was in the hospital, and I talked to a lady at the hospital who said she was a nursing assistant. She said she was doing that to decide whether or not she wanted to go to nursing school. I talked to David about it and he encouraged me. Larry Sylvia, Mary Jean Borst and I went and took the nurses' aid course for six weeks. That was probably in 1989. Part of the course was at the hospital and then all three of us went to work at Hillcrest Baptist Medical Center as nurses' assistants. We worked in different areas.

Several months into it, David asked Larry and Jean and some other people to come out to California. David was back and forth between California and Mount Carmel. He had a crew of people out in California who had bought a big house in Pomona.

Larry and Jean quit at Hillcrest, but I kept on working there as a nurses' assistant. Jeannine Bunds was a Registered Nurse and she worked there. I worked several months as a nurses' assistant and I worked the evening shift from 3:00 p.m. to 11:00 p.m. I had to give up my job at Mount Carmel as food buyer and coordinator for the kitchen; Novellette took that over.

I liked what I was doing at Hillcrest but I wasn't making much money. It only paid about $4.00 an hour and I had always been a good money earner from cleaning. I talked to David about going to nursing school and he said, oh yeah. It was late in the season and really was a little too late to apply, because they had practically chosen all the ones to be accepted, but I went ahead and went through all of the formalities and even went over to McLennan Community College to take one of the tests. They accepted me into the nursing program. I was forty-seven years old.

I went to McLennan Community College in Waco. The nursing program started in August 1990, but the summer before that they told me I needed to take an English course and a Math course. So I had to take an English language comprehension course. I went to school that summer and took the courses I needed for the nursing program. It stressed me out a lot because I had quit school in the eighth grade and it had been years since I had gone to school. The classes were going so fast and I didn't know things, but I made it through. As a matter of fact, my English teacher—and English was never my good subject—complimented me on how well I did on my final essay. I made it through the courses that summer and I started the nursing program in August. The following April, around Passover time, Dana Okimoto, one of David's wives, had a baby. I helped Jeannine deliver her baby, Jared (Scooter), at Mount Carmel.[65]

David had been coming to my house at different times, talking to Roy and me, saying that he wanted to tear down all of the houses at Mount Carmel and that he wanted to build one big house so people wouldn't have to go out in winter time when it was raining and muddy to come and eat and attend studies. He said, "I would like to have a place where they can all be in one building. I would like to have a place where people can come and visit for Bible studies." He was talking about that and he would put in other little remarks like, "You know, just because people leave the message, doesn't mean they're lost." As I think about it later, I realize that David was preparing the way for us to leave; we weren't supposed to be there as things developed the next year or so.

BONNIE AND ROY LEAVE MOUNT CARMEL

I was resenting a lot of things because I was busy with school and there were a few things that happened. I was unhappy with Roy and I felt as if I had been pushed into going back to him. I was all wound up about school. I had a lot of different people helping me study. Graeme Craddock[66] and John McBean, Janet McBean's brother,[67] helped me a lot with my studies. We had our house at Chandler to worry about. There were a lot of different reasons I was frustrated. I was being pulled in two different directions and I think David knew that. He had always told people: Just because somebody leaves here, as long as they don't put down the message, they're not lost. Everyone is free to leave.

It seemed like every time David would come out of the house at least five or six people followed him. He couldn't go anywhere by himself, especially because of some of the girls.

I was having to put up with a lot of jealousy from Roy. He was jealous of every guy there, even the young guys. They called me Mama. The guys liked me, but I felt more like their mama than their girlfriend. Roy was showing a lot of jealousy. I think he left once.

It was just a lot of stress, so I got to feeling that we needed to leave. I told Roy in April '91 that I thought we needed to leave. One of the girls I went to nursing school with told me there was a house for rent on the corner of 25th and Proctor. I told Roy about it. I went and looked at it, and we rented that little house. We were planning on leaving.

The next day I went down to the kitchen at Mount Carmel and Cyrus was there. As I was walking back Cyrus said, "Daddy wants to see you." I had always thought that when I finished nursing school I was going to get to go out to California and help deliver all of the babies that were supposed to be born. That was my plan. I was going to get away from Texas. I can't remember exactly what David said, but he asked, "Do you want to go to Dallas to work?" I wish I could remember everything he said, but with all of those people around I said,

"I don't want to go to Dallas to work. I thought I was going to California." He said, "No, we need somebody in Dallas to work." Well there wasn't anything relating to the Branch Davidians in Dallas. I don't remember exactly how he said it but he said something about my leaving, or "Maybe you ought to just leave." I wish there was someone who could tell me exactly what he said. It upset me because I knew that I had already gone and rented a house. I guess I was sneaking out. I had put a lot of stuff in the trunk of the car already. But what he said really upset me. I was upset about some things anyway and all of those people were standing around. He just made me feel like crap, which he could at times.

As I look back I can see how things progressed and that it was God's will that we not be there. I think David wanted us to leave because I think he knew down the road what was going to happen. He already said he wanted to tear all of the houses down and I just don't think he wanted Mama and Daddy around. Who knows what God told him to do, but I think it was working up to that, because it just wasn't meant for us to be there.[68]

The next morning I got up and went to school and I didn't go back. Roy moved our things over to the house. I don't know if David talked to Roy or not, or if Roy talked to him. I think God had His hand in our leaving.

After Roy and I moved I think David had Steve, or someone, call me one day. Something was said about some money and I said, "You have my refrigerator and my freezer." I said something about how I had brought my refrigerator and freezer down there for them to use and that was fine. I don't even remember exactly what was said. I don't know, but I was probably hurt. The next thing I know, here comes Steve and

Peter Hipsman with this brand-new, doublewide refrigerator. They said, "David wants you to have this." I said, "I don't want it." I didn't want it because I thought it was like a slap in the face. They couldn't get it in the house anyway. They tried to get it in the front door, and then they tried to get it in the back door. I told them to take it back to the store. Roy said, "Bonnie, you know if these guys go back with that refrigerator, they'll get in trouble." So I said, "Ya'll just leave it." I meant to call Sears to have them come pick it up because I wasn't trying to get David to replace my refrigerator. He took it wrong and I don't remember what I said or what provoked me to say what I said but he was trying to replace my refrigerator and freezer. I told all of my friends it was a graduation present from David, which it wasn't.

The refrigerator sat out on the patio for a long time. I called and told Sears I didn't want it but they never came and got it. Roy said it's just sitting there so we should bring it in. The refrigerator I had bought for the house wasn't working well or it quit working so we brought the new one into the house. We had to take the door off to get it into the house. It was so big in that little kitchen. That might have been in May or June 1991.

I graduated from nursing school in August, and then I went to work in Waco so we didn't move back to Chandler until March. I got a job at the nursing home in Chandler and they wanted me there in March, so I had a job lined up there. We told the guy, Dave, who was renting our house to move out. The house was a mess. We had to come in and rip out the carpet and paint. I had two weeks to do all of that before I went back to work. So it was in March of 1992 when we moved back down here.

Roy had turned sixty-two around the time he moved to Mount Carmel. He worked most of the time he was in Chandler. When he turned sixty-two he started drawing Social Security and we were getting $350 a month rent from this house, so that's what we lived on. Then when I got out of school I went to work in Waco. I worked there just a few months, from August to March.

Roy said he had been working all of his life and so he never worked any more jobs after he was sixty-two. He did a few little part-time jobs. He worked around Mount Carmel. He would drive the tractor, and do all of the bushhogging, and he cut the trails around the lake. When we moved back to our house in Chandler he had his hands full.[69] He had some odd jobs, but he never worked a regular job after that. Roy died August 31, 2001. This August will be three years.[70] He would have been seventy-three if he had lived twenty more days.

Anyway, we moved back to Chandler. Roy had a lot to do. He still had a tractor here. I went to work for Chandler Nursing Center in March. In July of '92 I found a job doing private duty nursing over at Edom. It's about sixteen miles from here. I was doing private duty work taking care of a lady, Kathy, who had been in a plane crash. I liked my job at the Chandler Nursing Center. I wasn't really looking for a job, but I think that God knew that with all that was going to happen in 1993 I needed a different job. I can look back and see that God led me there because that was the perfect place for me to be during the ATF raid, the fifty-one days of the FBI siege, and even after the fire. I didn't go back to work from April 19th[71] until August. I wasn't paid during that time, but Terry, Kathy's husband, gave me all of that time off. He had been through a tragedy with his wife, and he knew that I needed time to heal and work things out. We had a wonderful staff of nurses who pitched in and took up the slack while I was off from work so long.

I really think God leads us. I can remember asking Clive one time, "How can you keep up your faith?" and he said we can always look back and see how God has led us in the past and how God has directed our ways and has opened things up. I had liked my job at the Chandler Nursing Center, but that would not have been a good place for me to be during all of that in '93. Terry was very sympathetic. He was a strong person. His wife was in that Delta flight that crashed in Dallas in 1985. It hit a wind shear and crashed and she was one of the last survivors found. He quit work and took care of her, he never left her side for a year. She was totally dependent on him. She was a quadraplegic. She had to be fed through a tube. We had to do everything for her. He took such good care of her. That was my job for four years. It was a good place for me to be until she died in December 1995.

VISITS BACK AND FORTH WITH FOLKS AT MOUNT CARMEL

Reestablishing Contact

Roy and I moved back to Chandler in March of '92. In the following October, I was lying on the bed one day, on a Saturday I think, and I got a phone call. It was Clive's daughter, Shari. She said, "Hi Bonnie." I said, "Who's this?" She said, "Shari." I said, "Shari who?" "Shari Doyle." She said, "How are you doing?" I said, "I'm doing fine. What a nice surprise!" David had told her to call. She put Rachel on the phone and,

I think, Novellette, and several of them. They asked when I was going to come down and visit and why hadn't I been back? I didn't know what to say. I don't remember if I talked to David then or if there was another call later. I spoke with David either that time or when I got another call from Rachel and they invited me to come down. For some reason or another I couldn't go. He said, "I'm going to send Rachel." I asked, "Will you send the kids?" Of course he didn't. He sent Rachel and Novellette and Sherri Jewell. And Rachel brought Bobbie Lane, my newest grandbaby who I had not seen yet.

They came up and visited. When they called David and said they were going to leave my house to come back he said, "Oh no, it's late. Ya'll spend the night." So they spent the night and I got up the next morning and cooked a real big breakfast and we all ate like pigs. We had such a good time. That's when I took my last picture of Novellette. Rachel wouldn't let me take Bobbie's picture because David was funny about picture taking—had been for a long time. She wouldn't let me take a picture of them without David's permission, so I got Novellette's picture anyway. Then they went on home.

Roy and I went to Mount Carmel and visited the next time I had a weekend off. By then they only had the one big building to live in. All of the other houses had been torn down.

I think I had about twelve grandbabies there by that time. Of course that wasn't something David talked about much, but I could look around and see.

We went several times. When we went the first time we stayed in a front room on the first floor down the hall from the foyer by the front doors. This was a room they had originally fixed up for Trudy Meyers, a German woman in her 90s who came to Mount Carmel with Jean Borst and Ofelia Santoyo from California. David had bought her a nice bedroom set and dresser and they fixed the room up real nice with carpet. At that time Trudy was living over in David Jones's mobile home with Ofelia's mother, Concepción Acuña, and Edna Doyle and Mary Belle Jones, so Roy and I got to stay in that room. I knew to take water and things I needed with me to Mount Carmel. I think we stayed two nights. We spent the weekend. Everyone was glad to see us. The grandkids just followed us around everywhere: Cyrus, Star, Dayland, Serenity. And there were a lot of babies around.

We had a really nice time and they showed us all over the place. David took Roy up the stairs to the gunroom and showed him all the guns. I didn't see them. Roy saw them and he told me about all of these guns that were collector's items. A lot of them were in cases. I wasn't interested in guns. We probably had a Bible study and watched a movie.

I noticed on that first visit that they had provisions stacked everywhere. They had made a lot of changes. The cafeteria was arranged differently, and they had brought water in there, and they had electricity. And the grandkids, well, I just couldn't get out of their sight. I'd go here and I'd go there and they would be right behind me. I went up to the third story. On the far right side of the building when you went up to the third story in the tower, there was a big room where Novellette, Sherri Jewel and the girl from California stayed.[72]

Robyn Bunds wasn't at Mount Carmel. She had left before Roy and I left. She was out in California and she had taken Shaun. Her mother, Jeannine, didn't leave until after I had left, and then Dana Okimoto left with her two sons, Sky and Scooter, sometime after I had left. They had both moved to California.

I remember that Lisa Farris,[73] Novellette, Diana Henry,[74] and Sherri Jewel, and I were all ganged up upstairs. There were probably five or six girls staying upstairs in the attic room. I climbed up the ladder, and here came the grandkids! Cyrus and Star just tailed me everywhere I went. I loved having the kids with me and wanting to be with me. I was telling Novellette and the girls that I was going to come back one of these days, when the time was right, and they told me, "Stay where you're at. You're better off." They didn't elaborate or anything. They just said, "Stay where you are." On our walks they told me that some men were living across the road at the front of the property, who were supposed to be students. But they knew they weren't. They were all older and they drove really nice cars, not the kind of cars that students would be driving. They told me that helicopters were coming over all of the time.[75] David might have told me that, but I didn't get to spend much time with David. He was always busy, or off somewhere, or giving a long talk or giving Bible studies. I remember Robert Rodriguez coming over the last time I was there.[76]

Last Visit with David

We went two or three different times to visit. The last visit was sometime in January 1993. We went there on a Friday. I had worked all Thursday night, 7:00 p.m. to 7:00 a.m. Then we went down there. I had been up all day and on top of that I had a bad cold. Then at Mount Carmel we stayed up all night watching movies and eating popcorn and David gave a Bible study.

By that time they didn't have the guest bedroom anymore. They had converted it to a sewing room. They had sewing machines in there and the girls showed me the hunting vests they were making. The guys were taking them to the gun shows to sell.[77] Since there wasn't any place at Mount Carmel for us to sleep, Roy and I had a motel room in town. Roger was at Mount Carmel, too, at that time.

When we went and visited Cyrus that day, he said, "Grandma, Daddy says that if you loved us you would come back." I said, "We do love you Cyrus and I'm going to come back someday when the time is right."

Anyway it was late. It was about midnight. I was tired, I was sick, so I told Roy, "Let's go." I went out to the car and David called Roy back into the front room. There were some guys in there and they were talking about something. I was getting really irritated and tired, so I went in and told Roy, "Come on, let's go. I'm tired." David said something to me and I called him Vernon and we had words. I think I was just stretched to the limit from being sick and tired. We went out and I said, "I'm leaving." I never usually acted that way. I went and got in the car and David told me to never come back. I think that was the last time I saw him.

Before David and I had words, I remember that after the meeting had broken up we were standing there in the foyer and there was a piano in the hall. The stairs were there. I hugged Rachel, Cyrus, Star, and Bobbie and all of them. We were all hugging. I can just see them. David was standing there before they went up to bed. I went out to the car but then David said, come here, Daddy, I want to show you something or talk to you about something. I went out to the car and Roy stayed, so I went back in to get him. That's the way I remember it. I guess I was irritated. I see now how God worked things out so we wouldn't be there later on.

Roy and I went to the motel. Roger stayed at Mount Carmel. Roy drove back out there the next morning to pick up Roger, and the kids ran out to say hi to him and Rachel called them back in. David made comments two or three times that he was worried that Roy would kidnap the kids, which was unfounded. He wouldn't have. David wasn't mad at Roy and Roy wasn't mad at David.

That was the last time I visited Mount Carmel and my feelings were hurt. David had told me several times that I wore my feelings on my shirt sleeve. Then it wasn't long before the ATF raid on February 28, 1993.

THE ATF RAID, FEBRUARY 28, 1993

On Saturday, February 27, my friend Billie called me late in the evening and said, "Bonnie, what's going on in Waco?" I said, "I don't know." She said, "I got the paper today and there is a big article, 'The Sinful Messiah,' and it's all about your son."[78] It worried me so I turned right around and called David. I hadn't talked to him since that little thing. I called David and he said, "Hi, Mama." I said, "Hi, David, how are you?" "Oh, I'm fine, Mama." I said, "I heard about this article." He said, "Oh, it's nothing." I said, "You're sure?" I asked him if he wanted to send Rachel and the kids to my house in case something happened. He said, "Oh no, no, no, no. I'm not sending my family anywhere. It's fine. Why don't you come down here?" I said, "It's my weekend to work. I'm fixing to go to work." It was Saturday night. He said, "Everything is fine. I'm not sending my kids or Rachel anywhere. There's no problem. God will take care of us." And he said, "When are you coming, Mama? When are you going to come see us?" I said, "I'm working this weekend, so maybe next weekend we can come."

I went off to work and the next morning was Sunday. I got home about 7:30 a.m. and I went to bed. It was about 10:30 a.m. when my phone rang. My sister in-law, Jackie, called and said, "Bonnie, get up and turn your TV on. Something is going down at Waco." I remember that's how she said it: "Something is going down at Waco." So I got up and turned on the TV set and saw all of this shooting and everything. I ran out the back door. Roy was out on the tractor cutting grass. I started screaming, "Roy! Roy! Roy!" I guess he heard me because he came running. He came in and we started watching it on the TV.[79]

I went to work that night. That was Sunday morning and I was supposed to work Sunday night. Phyllis, the head house-keeper, and Terry, my boss, were there. They had heard about what was happening so I went ahead and told them, "That's my son." I went to work that night and I was off the next day, on Monday.

On Monday my phone was ringing and the media were here and all kinds of crap was going on. Snuggles my little dog and Blackie had just had puppies. Someone left the gate open and I saw my puppies running out. They were little so I ran out front to grab the puppies and I went around to the back of the house to put them in the pen. I was outside when the phone rang about 9:30 or 10:00 a.m. As I came inside the answer machine was just going off. During the time I had gone out David had called me and left me a message on my machine. I had been trying to call him but I couldn't get through. I couldn't get through to David after that and I guess he never could call me, so all I have is that message that he left.[80]

I was off on Monday and Tuesday, so we went to Waco. I had to come back to go to work on Wednesday and Thursday, but then I was off that weekend. So we loaded up and went back to Waco. Things happened so fast, the lawyers all started coming down offering to do things *pro bono*. Different things were happening, and we went down. Dick DeGuerin was there.[81] The federal agents wouldn't let us into Mount Carmel. We stayed in the Motel 6 in Bellmead.[82]

THE SIEGE

I lost track of time, but the siege was fifty-one days.[83] I don't think I took any time off from work other than my weekends. Most of the time I was off, we were in Waco.

I hired Dick DeGeurin to represent David. I was told about Dick DeGeurin through someone who said Dick would be willing to defend David if I called him and asked. So I called Dick DeGuerin and hired him. I liked him right away. He was a very nice person. He went in to see David five times during the fifty-one days. He has a letter that David wrote saying that they would come out. He was very impressed with David and all the people he met inside Mount Carmel. They fixed him and Jack Zimmerman[84] a meal. They fixed them a meal and brought them basins of water to wash their hands in and showed them around. Dick and Jack talked with some of the kids. Dick was really impressed with what he saw inside. During the siege I never got to go see David or talk to him, but Dick was always available for me to talk to any time I needed to. We spent a lot of time together, Dick, his wife Janie, and I.

I met a lot of people during those fifty-one days. All the reporters wanted an interview. I had some good times and I had some bad times, but it was kind of exciting with some of those reporters in Waco trying to find us. One of them almost had a wreck just trying to get away from another one. It was really funny. We had some good times because we had to get our minds off of things.

I tried to get custody of the kids to get them out. David had written the letter and said that they were going to come out.[85] I went around to Child Protective Services and told them I wanted to make arrangements for when the kids came out. I wanted to be able to take care of my grandkids so that they wouldn't have to go with strangers. I went to the nursing school and talked to my teachers to get them to write recommendations for me.

During this time all of these movie people came around and they paid me to do some things. A guy came from Hollywood and had us sign a contract; they were going to make a movie. They wrote the script and paid us about $10,000 to do the movie. I lived on that money for a while after the fire, because Terry told me to take off all the time I needed. That's how I lived without any salary. The movie never got made. The script was very good, but I was told that the government wouldn't let them make the movie. The government controls a lot of stuff that goes on in Hollywood and they never let it be made. Warner Brothers wanted to do it but they couldn't sell it to anyone. No one wanted to carry it.

With the movie I thought I was going to have money to take care of the kids. We were looking at getting a little bit bigger house and I was doing everything I could to get the kids so I could take care of them while their parents were in jail. I thought that eventually the mothers would get out, but then the fire happened.

THE FIRE, APRIL 19, 1993

I remember praying that Monday morning as I drove to work. I pray all the time, but that was my time for prayer. I was praying, "God, this is what I'm trying to do. They are your children. Can they come out if possible so I can take care of the kids?" I was getting Kathy's meds ready at 6:00 in the morning when I saw on television the tanks starting to tear down the building.[86] I called people right away. I called Roy first and then I called Dick DeGuerin. Dick DeGuerin was on his way to Denton, Texas for a trial and he turned around and went back to Waco. John Feist, my friend with *A Current Affair*, was on his way home to San Antonio and he turned around and came straight here to see me that evening.[87] I went home and Roy and I watched what was happening at Mount Carmel on television. About noon we saw the fire. It was just a hectic day. It was terrible.

I don't know if it was that evening or the next morning, but we went to Waco and met with Dick DeGuerin and his wife Jane in a hotel. He just cried. I cried. Everybody cried.

I don't remember too much after that. I was sort of numb.[88]

1994 CRIMINAL TRIAL

I didn't go to the criminal trial in San Antonio. I had already taken off work from April 19th until about the middle of August. My boss was very good to let me off during that time.

When the trial started, Dick DeGuerin or someone told me that I would probably be called as a witness, but I never was. I had already been told that the witnesses were not allowed to be in the courtroom. I was trying not to miss a lot of work again, not so much because of the monetary aspect of it, but because my being off earlier had inconvenienced the other nurses. They had doubled up the shifts all the months I was off.

I was just waiting to be told when to come to the trial, so I never did make it down to San Antonio. I know some people who were there who didn't get to go into the courtroom, and they were never called.[89]

2000 CIVIL TRIAL

What happened at the civil trial is pretty much what I expected, considering we had Walter Smith for the judge.[90] After all the depositions, and the running to Waco for hearings, and this and that and everything, I actually wasn't able to be at all of the trial, but my husband Roy was. He went over there and stayed. I had to work so I was only there for several days. The outcome was about what I expected.

Ramsey Clark had been sick. He looked bad, and he didn't even get to speak much. I think the whole thing was a farce. The jury wasn't even a jury of twelve, and they never even came back after they reached their verdict. That's all right. There will be another trial some day. There will be another judge some day, a heavenly one.

The wrongful death lawsuit wasn't about money. It really wasn't. I was hoping for someone higher up to admit some wrongdoing, mistakes, and apologize or something.[91] Of course no amount of money could bring our families back. It's been eleven years now.[92] It has pretty much consumed all our lives. Sometimes I'd just like to forget the whole thing. Of course you can't forget it.

I was a little disappointed at the appeal in New Orleans.[93] Probably more disappointed in that, but in a way, it was what I expected, too. Then the appeal to the Supreme Court was turned down, also.[94] They didn't want to even hear it.

It's a sad thing that happened at Mount Carmel and people aren't going to admit to it. There's nothing you can do about it. You can't change it.

LIFE AFTER THE FIRE

Some Travels

After the fire Dick DeGuerin cried real tears. He was very upset about the whole situation. He's a very good person. He and Janie invited Roy and me down to their ranch. He had a ranch where they went to get away on the weekends. It's not a huge place, but it's very unique. It's a real rustic looking place and they have fixed up a caboose for a guest room. It's really nice and peaceful.

We all made a trip to New York City together to be on *Good Morning America*. We had a good time in New York. Roger went with me. We had to get up at four o'clock in the morning because the show aired really early. Later on we walked all around Manhattan and bought those funny-looking hot dogs at the neatest little stands. They're different from what you get here. We had a good time. It was nice, walking down Central Park before we got on the plane and returned to Texas.

Experiences at Work

After 1993 I didn't always know how to let people know I am David's mother. When I was working as a private duty nurse taking care of a patient, everyone was just really, really nice to me there. My boss told me he didn't necessarily agree with what David had done, but they were very sympathetic. My patient died in December of '95. So then I was without a job for a couple months.

I never really encountered anyone, anywhere who was ugly or mean to me. I got an awful lot of mail, boxes of mail and letters, most of it very sympathetic. Two letters that I can think of were very derogatory and neither one of those people signed their names to them, which I thought was sort of cowardly.

I got letters from people all over the country. Some sent tapes. Some people sent cards. Many people just sent letters and sympathy. A few people sent checks. They are probably still in the envelopes. I never cashed any. They weren't large amounts.

I now work at a pediatric clinic. I had been there at least three years before anyone knew that I was David Koresh's mother. It was really funny. I came into work one morning and one of the nurses came up to me and said, "I saw you on TV last night."[95] She was very discrete about it. She asked, "You're David Koresh's mother?" I said, "I am." And she said, "I won't say anything to anybody." And I said, "That's fine. Nobody here knows it, and I appreciate that you're not talking about it." It wasn't that I was embarrassed or ashamed or anything. It was just there wasn't any reason to bring it up. I'd take off and go to Waco, and I'd talk about Waco, but no one ever made any connection with the Branch Davidians. It just wasn't the right time to say anything. But after she told me that, I thought about telling some people.

There was a Wellness Center where I worked out quite a bit, and a couple of the older men there had seen me on TV. I thought of a couple of people at work I wanted to tell. So I went in to work and the boss wasn't there that day, but one of the RN's was there. It was so funny. She still laughs about it. I went into the office and I said, "Beverly, I'd like to talk to you about something." And she said, "What are you going to tell me? That you're David Koresh's mother?" I said, "Yes." She went ten shades of red. She was just joking and she was so embarrassed. She said I looked so serious and she didn't know why she said that. She's not the type of person who would hurt anyone's feelings. So I explained to her who I was and a little bit about it, and I went to a couple of other people there, including my boss, because I knew that with this much stuff on TV it would eventually come out.

Maybe a week or so later, I came in and someone told me, "Hey, Julie told me that she saw you on TV." One of the office girls had seen one of the programs on television, on Arts and Entertainment or one of the other channels. They came to work talking about it and one of the nurse practitioners heard people discussing it and she put an end to it right there. She said, "We're not going to discuss this or talk about it. No gossip. If Bonnie wants to talk about it, fine. But we're not going to talk about it among ourselves." No one ever said a word to me after that. By then I had told several people and it was not like everyone didn't know.

Afterwards I joked with Dorlene, another nurse I worked with, about it. I was always dropping hints. I talked about my son being dead, about going to Waco all the time, and different things. She never did pick up on it. She laughed and said, "I don't know why I never picked up on it." She said it just never did click with her. She doesn't have a television and she doesn't read newspapers.

No one at work was ever ugly to me. Ever since then, when people ask questions, I have shown them "Rules of Engagement" or similar videos. Most of them were really enlightened by it. Most of them are working people. They weren't glued to their TVs so they didn't know a lot about it. Many of them didn't even read newspaper stories but just heard little bits about it. So the ones who watched those movies were really shocked and disgusted at what the federal agents did.

I was told that one of the patients had heard something one day and she called the clinic about it, saying that I had discussed it. I got called in and I said I had never, never discussed this with a patient. I said that I had just recently let some people at work know that I was David's mother. They said, well don't discuss it at work. I said okay. I never had anyway. I don't know how this person heard something unless it was something said out in the hall.

Overall everyone has been very nice. When people ask questions I answer them. I have never had anyone anywhere just be ugly to me. Most people are very understanding.

GOING BACK TO MOUNT CARMEL

After the fire it was a long time before they let anyone into the Mount Carmel property. They had a fence around it. I didn't go around there much during that time. I was back at work and everything had died down some. Different ones were coming onto the property, and things were happening over the years. Charlie Pace and his family moved onto the property.[96] Finally Edna and Clive put a mobile home there in '99. A couple of years later we built a little memorial building next door to their trailer. Quite a few people helped to build it. It was a fun experience to build that little memorial museum.[97]

People from Austin got together and did a radio show where a lot of people sent in contributions to build a chapel at Mount Carmel. Personally, I didn't particularly think we ought to build a chapel there, but I'm not the boss. Anyway, it isn't that big. It's a nice chapel. A lot of people came and worked on it, and spent a lot of money, and a lot of donations came in. We made a lot of friends and it is a nice place. It was completed in 2000. It's a good place to have a memorial every year on April 19th.[98] There's still some work that needs to be done on the chapel. The upstairs is not finished and there are a few things that need to be done, but it is a nice place for visitors to come to worship and to have the memorials.

Attendance at memorials has dwindled a little bit over the years. They're not quite as big and the media don't show up liked they used to. In one sense, I think that's good.

Most of the memorials have been very good. We've had some good speakers come. I think it was around the eighth year that Dick DeGuerin came back. That was the first time he'd come back since the fire. He came with the other attorney, Mr. Zimmerman, who was Steve Schneider's attorney in 1993.[99] Mr. Zimmerman and his wife are very nice people. Of course, Janie came with Dick DeGuerin. Every year except one year, Ramsey Clark has come, and he usually has several people with him. He has always been a central figure in all our memorials. The same group comes every year as well as some new people. The smallest crowd has been about a hundred people.[100]

The memorials were all very nice. We had a service, speakers, and we read all the names of the people who died on February 28th and April 19th, including the names of the ATF agents. Some years a man named David Hall brought a Liberty Bell and we rang it for each name. Each memorial has been a little bit different. It's a good thing to have, I think. It's just sad that we had the Oklahoma City bombing in 1995. It was especially sad to have something tragic like that happen on the same day we were having our memorial.[101]

I'd like to see a park at Mount Carmel, a place where people can visit, and a bigger museum, maybe even take the chapel and make that the museum.[102] There are a lot of interesting things that could be put in the museum for people to be able to see. We'd need a caretaker to take care of it. I think it's a beautiful piece of property. I'd like to see it more like it was before. I'd like to see the cemetery cleaned up with a fence put around it and kept up. You've got five or six people buried in there right now.[103]

The cemetery has in it Anna Hughes, the little old lady that George Roden dug up. David Bunds and his wife have a baby buried there. Someone else has a baby buried there. Edna Doyle is buried there. Trudy Meyers and Tilly Friesen are buried there. The cemetery is out on a corner of the property. It would be nice to have some headstones marking the graves.

A lot of people come out to Mount Carmel now. People from all over the world come in their motor homes to see it, so there are a lot of visitors. I wish that it could be fixed up more like a park with some benches put around and a few trees planted and a little bit more shade somewhere, maybe even a pavilion built with a top on it because it gets awfully hot. The wind blows all the time.

REMEMBERING THE PEOPLE AND LIFESTYLE AT MOUNT CARMEL

I lived with the Branch Davidians from August of 1985 until April of 1991. When I first met a lot of those people in '81 I fell in love with all of them. I loved their simple way of life, their simple diet, trying to be away from things.

We moved back to Mount Carmel from the Palestine camp in 1988. It was just like one big family. We had the kids playing and we had worship. On Sabbath we usually had worship from 9:00 a.m. until 12:00. Then we'd stop and have lunch. We'd eat again in the evening. We had the Daily every day. The rest of the time, we'd go to town and do the laundry at the washateria. We had to do grocery shopping. Since there weren't very many cars a lot of people had to go to town at the same time. Someone was always running to town to take people to do errands or to the doctor or the chiropractor or whatever was needed. The kids played and all the women kept their own houses. In the evenings we often had exercise class. I remember Jaydean Wendel was the first exercise leader. Some of us would go down to the church and we'd exercise. We were just like a big old extended family.

At first we didn't have TV. David did get a big screen TV later on and then we'd watch movies. We'd cook big meals and the girls would get in there and make cookies. At that time we didn't use a lot of the things that make it easy to cook. We didn't cook with mixes. If we made cakes or cornbread we beat our egg whites to fluff them up. We had some good cooks. They loved to experiment. I guess pizza was our favorite meal. We would make it every once in a while—big old pans of pizza from scratch. Other than that, I guess in the summer our favorite food was popcorn and watermelon. We all loved to eat.

Every once in a while we'd have a hoe down. Not very often, but we'd get in the big building and David and some of them would play music and we'd just sing and dance. Not dance in the way you do in a nightclub. Everyone did their own little thing, especially Perry and Catherine. They would be so funny. They'd get out there and dance and just had a good time. It was good, clean fun, with the kids running up and down. You didn't have to worry about kids when they went out and played because there wasn't any traffic. It was just nice.

The women would take walks. Certain ones would walk after supper. We'd get out and walk around the lake. From my front door, all the way to the lake, and back up the road was exactly one mile. Novellette and I and my grandkids walked together. Cyrus and Star were always walking with me. It was nice around on the other side of the lake. It was really pretty over there. There were some willow trees growing up and someone had made a little pier you could walk out on.

I think food cost $30 or $35 a month per person. For a family of three that was $90 a month. There were a few people living there who probably didn't have money, but I don't know who did and who didn't have money. Most of the people had some kind of an income. We had some retired people there. I know Henry and Gertrude Chang used to pay extra money. They'd pitch in a lot. We always had plenty of money and plenty to eat.

We would buy very frugally. We tried to buy things that were on sale, and we ate a lot of fruits and vegetables. We'd buy apples by the cases, and also potatoes and onions. I remember there was a time we made our own mayonnaise in blenders. We ordered oatmeal, beans, brown rice, from the co-op out of Arkansas and we used nutritional yeast flakes. We bought that in a fifty-pound bag. We ate a lot of popcorn. Everyone loved popcorn. There might have been a couple of people who wouldn't eat it, but we had popcorn just about every night. We'd have soup or fruit salad with it or watermelon or maybe just a few bananas. We bought bananas galore. Supper was always the lightest meal. Breakfast was very good and lunch was substantial. We had meat once in a while. For a long time we were vegetarians; later we'd have meat once in a while but not all the time. We ate very well, very healthy. There was always plenty. There was never a time when we didn't have something to eat and money to buy food.

Even though we had separate houses, we cooked and ate communally. Sheila Martin did some cooking in her house. She had to have special things for Jamie, so she had cooking facilities in her house. Most of us didn't even have a stove. We just had a wood stove for heat. I don't think we had refrigerators. I had one in my house for a short time. I didn't have it in there for very long. I think we put it back when we got the storeroom fixed. We stored a lot of extra stuff in the refrigerator from the kitchen—cheese and things like that. We bought a lot of cheese and yogurt.

There were some good cooks who made loads of vegetarian dishes. I had a millet loaf recipe that people really loved.

I learned it from a lady in California: add millet and tomato juice and black olives and onions. It was good. They cooked millet a lot for breakfast. We served it with tahini and honey. We also had oatmeal for breakfast, and some mornings we had eggs.

We didn't necessarily have a bookkeeper, but for the most part someone was in charge of the shopping. At one time Perry Jones used to do the shopping, but then David took him off that and put Novellette in charge. Novellette would collect the money every month, and do the grocery shopping. She kept a record when people gave her money and she gave them a receipt.

We didn't have a water bill. Everyone had their own electricity. Perry probably took care of the electric bill on the church and stuff. I paid the electric bill for my house and my phone bill. I guess Perry paid his. Catherine got a check, so she must have paid hers. Most people had electricity. At first there were some houses that didn't have electricity. For a while I let the girls run a big, long, heavy-duty extension cord from my house so they could have lamps. I think they eventually got electricity in there when Jeannine moved in. We made do.

I remember it got awfully hot at Mount Carmel. No one had air conditioning. We did have fans. I remember lying in my little house with the fan on me to take a nap. It wasn't so bad at night.

So many of the young people today don't know how to rough it. I had a little bit of experience roughing it because we had camped out. And, growing up, I had lived in houses that didn't have bathrooms or even water. When my kids were little we had well water, and I was always having to conserve water. So living at Palestine or even at Mount Carmel wasn't so hard on me because I knew how to conserve water. I knew how to take a bath with a gallon of water, wash my hair with it, too, and still be clean. People stayed clean even though we didn't have a lot of water.

David bought one of those great big round tanks and it was on a trailer. Roy would pull it over to the water company at Beaver Lake, which was about three or four miles away, and we'd pay to fill that thing up with water because our well wasn't working. Roy brought it back and parked it. Everyone went down and filled their water jugs.

At Palestine, we didn't have any outhouses or bathrooms but we would go out in the woods and dig a hole. Actually we'd string off a place back in the woods. We'd take a long piece of string and someone would start off by digging a hole. Then we'd go down and empty our bucket, cover that hole up and dig another one for the next person. The next person would cover theirs in the hole and dig a hole for the next person. The shovel would always be left there. It was smart. Of course that east Texas sand was easy. It was not like having to dig mud or hard dirt. At Mount Carmel the soil was completely different. It was that old hard black stuff. We didn't empty buckets there. Mount Carmel had a septic system that still worked so we could use the toilets in the houses and save all our water in the tub from showers to flush the toilet. Most people had that. It was pretty easy to do. It wasn't as rustic at Mount Carmel. When they first built at Mount Carmel they had running water.[104]

I'm sure it was easier than the pioneers had it. At least we could run to the store and get things! I'm thankful for the experiences I had there. I really am.

We used lanterns and flashlights and candles a lot even though a lot of us had electricity. Some houses didn't. David always stressed to everyone to be very careful. One night we were having a meeting in the building and Cyrus looked out the window and said, "There's a fire! There's a fire!" I think this was during Passover time because we had a lot of visitors then and some people were using the rooms in Sister Roden's house. Someone had left a candle burning and the wind had blown the curtain into it. If Cyrus hadn't looked out and seen it, we would never have known it. A lot of people ran over there. I think Brother Lawter was asleep and we woke him up and got him out and were able to save some of the people's things that were in the house. It just went "whoosh." Cyrus saw that. The house burned to the ground. It was a good-sized house, too.

David didn't coordinate things because he was always busy. Much of the time he was in California. He stayed with the Bunds a while before they moved to Mount Carmel. There were always some people out in California. We had the house in San Bernadino. Then they bought the house in Pomona. I never did see that house. There were two households. Perry Jones was out there, so I guess Perry took care of paying the rent and the bills and everything. For a while I was in charge of buying for the kitchen. I handled the money and kept a record of it. I don't think David spent any time paying bills. David would appoint someone to do that. Perry Jones was the one who was mostly in charge. David always said that when he wasn't there Perry was in charge. If you needed something you went to Perry.

At Mount Carmel Novellette handled the grocery money. When Novellette was gone to Florida, I took care of the grocery money. When I went to nursing school David said it was too much for me so he handed it back over to Perry. He might have given it back to Novellette. It was a big job.

It all worked so smoothly. Everyone got along. We would make a schedule for each week for who was going to work in the kitchen. There were certain ones who liked to and then there were some who just weren't any good in the kitchen. We didn't want them in it. There were some people David wouldn't allow in the kitchen. Sheila and Ofelia[105] and Bonnie might be in the kitchen for breakfast one week. Sometimes the ones who did breakfast did lunch, too. Then someone else would do supper. Then it would be someone else the next week. We changed it around. The young girls would always help with the dishes. I think we fixed up dishpans with hot water and let people wash their own dishes. Of course we still had the cooking dishes and all that to clean up. Everything was cleaned and swept up when we got through. We may not have had real nice floors but we kept them clean.

When I moved to the Palestine camp in '85 I don't think there was more than thirty people. Then, as more and more people came in, it grew. I guess probably at any given time after we got back to Mount Carmel there might have been as many as sixty people on a regular basis. We got everybody together at Passover time. People came over from England and different places. We might have had a hundred and fifty, maybe even two hundred people at times. A lot of people had been there for years. The kids were born into it. But as time went on and more and more people joined or came, the attraction was mainly that they wanted to study.[106]

A lot of them came from different places and they'd meet David and then they came to Mount Carmel to study. No one will tell you they loved the living conditions. It was probably pretty hard on some of them. I was raised up poor so I've lived every which way you can. I know the main thing that attracted the adults was what they heard from David in the studies. That's why they came and that's why they stayed. It certainly wasn't the houses or the food or anything. It was exciting. I mean it was interesting. I'm not saying I exactly went there for the message. It was a place for me to go because I was leaving home, although I did like the people and I was listening.

I'd say that all the people from Hawaii and different ones from California and Australia came because they had heard David teaching and they wanted to hear more. A lot of them gave up homes and family to come. They gave up businesses. David could open that Bible and make it correlate, chapter after chapter after chapter. It made sense. I can hear someone go through it now and I can't get anything out of it. I can't repeat a lot of the stuff he taught, but I saw him sit for hours and give a study and fall off to sleep and doze for five or ten minutes and wake up and take up right where he left off. He could talk. I'd get tired sometimes. There were some people I don't care how long he talked or if he told them to go to bed, they'd still keep hanging around. Catherine was one of those.

David was a night person. He might call a meeting and it could go on and on and on and on and then he'd say, "Ya'll had enough? Everybody go to bed." Some people would get up and go to their houses, but there were always the ones hanging around. A lot of times he'd just start in with another study. Some people were afraid that if they went home they were going to miss something.

To see how everyone lived at Mount Carmel was just amazing. They were very generous with the kids. They loved the kids. We all worked together. To have that many people—one hundred to two hundred and fifty people at a time—is a lot these days, but we all got along really well. We were all like one big happy family. It was just amazing and I know it was only God's will that allowed it.

REMEMBERING THE CHILDREN

Cyrus was my number one grandson. I've talked about him a little bit. I have lots of pictures of him. I remember the first time I saw that little guy. I thought, "A little stranger. Maybe I could get to like this little guy." And I did. It didn't take me long. To hear him say "Grandma" when he got big enough to talk—"Grandma, Grandma, Grandpa, Grandpa"—that was music to my ears. He spent a lot of time with me, especially after I went out to California. He and Rachel had been there for a while. He was getting to be almost one year old. I'd take him to K-Mart and different places and play with him and feed him popcorn. We had a really good time. I enjoyed him.

Cyrus had long curly blond hair. He had the Jones's hair. He didn't particularly like to have it brushed. Rachel would braid it a lot. David told him, "Son, you don't ever have to cut your hair unless you want to." David never wanted to cut his hair. Cyrus's hair was way down his back, and he had little freckles across his nose, and he would smile. Rachel would cut his bangs. He never had a haircut other than his bangs.

I remember that when I was going to nursing school Cyrus got so tickled when I would practice giving injections in an orange. I'd bring my needle home to practice, and he'd say, "I want to do that, Grandma. I want to do that. Can I give Grandpa a shot?" I slipped the needle out and let him take the syringe over and poke Roy. He thought he had given him a shot. He'd just laugh.

We lived several houses down from Rachel. Cyrus loved to come up to my house. I had a little patio in the back and he loved to hammer nails, so I'd give him hammer and nails and he'd get out there. Our firewood was usually on a slab, and he'd get out there and hammer and nail, hammer and nail. He came up one day and he said, "Grandma, my daddy said I can't come up here anymore if you don't spank me when I'm bad." I said, "Okay, don't you be bad Cyrus!" He did something one day, I don't know what it was, and I said, "Okay, Cyrus, come over here and get on my knee because I've got to spank you." So I spanked him. He went on and told his daddy. He wanted to make sure I spanked him so he could come back.

I have his little book in there in my trunk. It's a little book called, *Peace at Last*. Cyrus loved it. Roy would read to him more than I did because Roy used to read to Roger. Cyrus loved that book called *Peace at Last*, and Roy would read it over and over and over to him.

Then Star came along–David's daughter. She looked more like Rachel, but she had strawberry-blond hair. Cyrus used to get a lot of attention from all the young girls until Star came along. Then he didn't get as much attention. Then he was more mine. Star was more serious. As she got bigger, I guess I didn't spend as much time with her because the girls would play with her a lot. Cyrus was bigger and running around and he'd come to my house. I guess I was closer to him. You get attached to the first one. Star got a little bit bigger and then she started coming up to the house, too. They both loved for us to hold them and read to them. Star had such a sweet little smile. She was sort of quiet.

Then Serenity started coming up a lot. She was Michele's little girl, and she was real serene. David named all his children. He named her Serenity and she was a very serene little girl. She was sort of quiet, too.

Cyrus was the talker. Cyrus really took to Roy when Roy came to Mount Carmel. He loved his Grandpa. Roy would lie in bed and read to him. Cyrus used to want to spend the night with us. David used to let him stay once in a while, but not very often.

We had tea parties. The kids came up to the house and they had little chairs and a table. They came over and wanted me to make them tea and have a tea party. I have a picture with Cyrus, Star, and Joshua Sylvia,[107] drinking tea. I would make them a little mint tea or something with a little honey in it. Later on I would buy seltzer water, something like Perrier. I would pour that in a glass and put some lemon juice. I'd make it fizz to make them Sprite. We had soda drinks every once in a while but it wasn't something that was bought all of the time. David would treat them with Sprite every once in a while. But they had their little tea parties or Sprite parties at my house. We had a lot of good times.

When I brought gifts for the children, David said, "If you are going to buy things for Cyrus and Star and Bobbie, give it for everybody." I could go along with that. So when I baked cookies, I baked lots of cookies! David wanted to be fair in every way and like he said, they were God's children. They were special children to be raised in special ways and to be something special. And they *were* special kids. Those kids were not like your everyday kids.

I work in a pediatric clinic. I see kids who are spoiled and they're raised on junk food. I'm not saying our kids never had a little cry or a little act of self-will. They did occasionally. But most of the time when our kids came to breakfast they were ready to eat. Those kids enjoyed their food. They were happy. They didn't get cokes and ice cream and candy and junk food between meals. By the time lunch got there, the bell rang, and it was time to eat, they had hearty appetites and ate what was put before them.

I don't know why David had so many children. This is a subject I don't get into too much. I attended the Bible studies, but I don't remember the reason, but there was a reason for all of that. It's not something that I really understood or approved of. It was not something that was discussed or talked about. It was not even something that was done in an open manner. You didn't ask questions, you didn't make comments. It was a very private type of thing. As a matter of fact I was in California when I was told that Nicole's baby Dayland was in the hospital. I was upset and asked what was wrong. David said, "Mama, that's none of your business. That's God's child. They are God's children, and not your concern."

I've got to say those kids loved David. When Roy and I went back to Mount Carmel those few times and David had set up his musical equipment on that stage and played, the kids were always right there. Or if he came down from the stage, they would want to sit on his lap. Those kids all loved David.

I don't ever remember seeing David spank a child.[108] David told Daniel Martin one time that he was going to give him a lickin'. And he did. David took Daniel back to the storeroom where the freezer was and took out some ice cream and told him, "Okay, you lick this up now." It was so funny. He told him he was going to give him a lickin' but he didn't say a lickin' of what. Daniel never forgot that.

There was a paddling stick on the wall in the kitchen for the children. Most people had their own little wooden paddles, but they were really neat. They were flat like rice paddles. When children misbehaved, the mothers were usually the ones who took them back to the pantry and put them across their knees and told them why they were being disciplined. They would go back in private and just pat them on their little butts. They didn't leave bruises. And then they would love them.

The kids would correct us a lot of times. "You shouldn't be drinking that water with your meal." "Where's your slip? You're supposed to have a slip on." The kids were learning and they were righteous children. They didn't whine, "I don't want that, I want something else" or "I want to go to McDonald's" or "I don't want to go to bed." They were good kids.

Of course the kids were there because their parents were, but they'd all come to the studies. Everyone came. They were allowed to sit there and they listened a lot. Our kids learned a lot of good things. They were not like most of the kids you see. They didn't sit in front of the TV set for hours or eat junk food. They were smart. We had school classes for the children, too.

REMEMBERING DAVID

My mother helped me with both of my kids, all of her grand-kids really. My mom and dad were very important in David's upbringing. My daddy was a carpenter and David learned a lot of carpentry work from him. As he got older, David worked with him on several jobs. David spent a lot of time with him. My daddy was an avid fisherman and David loved fishing.

David was such a good little boy. When he got bigger he did smoke cigarettes and I'm sure he drank a few beers, but he was always searching and questioning, wanting to know "Why?" Why this and why that and how things worked.

I think being raised the way he was and being an illegiti-mate child he learned so much growing up. My first husband beat him on his butt and left it black and blue. I left him after a year and a half. I may have done some things that made David know Mama was not all that great. He had a step-dad, Roy, who was stern in some areas. David just knew about human nature and he loved his grandma. He loved people.

My mama took him to a Seventh-day Adventist church when he was four years old. He loved the kindergarten room. I remember that when I had him in church school in Dallas he took me into the chapel and he said, "Oh, Mama, isn't it beautiful and peaceful?" He was sixteen years old then but he had some sort of Spirit in him that most people don't have.

David learned the Bible mostly on his own. I never was a Bible student. I took him to church, but I went to church all my life and never learned the things he learned. There was something in him that wanted him to learn. He compre-hended what he read in the scriptures. That's why I feel that God led him and was using him. God taught him. It sure wasn't Mama. David had a yearning—a desire and need to learn the scriptures. He could say the scriptures the first time he ever went to church. I think God put some kind of Spirit in him to do that.

I don't see David as the Christ, Jesus Christ. I see David as being filled with the Spirit, as someone who was chosen to be a spokesman for God. I see David as the imperfect opposite of what Christ was, the perfect.[109] The way I look at it is that David was born into this world. I wasn't a virgin, I was young, but he was born and he grew up to be everything. I think God caused certain circumstances in his childhood for him to understand humanity. For instance, as far as disciplining children, he learned from all the wrong things I did how to do things right and to teach people to do things right.

David could look at a person and just read them like a book. He could talk to you and correct you in ways that you couldn't refute. It's just hard to explain. He was just very wise in human nature, and he certainly didn't learn it from his daddy or me.

I saw David many times stop people or people would ask him something, and he would talk to them on their level. He just seemed to say the right things. He knew no stranger. All the things he did were wise.

I remember one time when we were in California and we went into the grocery store to get something to eat and I picked up a grape and put it in my mouth, as people do. He said, "Don't ever do that. That's stealing. Don't do that." He counseled people to pay their taxes and be true to the government and do what we are supposed to do as good citizens.

So then people say, well he had all of his wives, and it is claimed that he was with underaged girls. But if you read the scriptures, David, Abraham, all of them had more than one wife. I tell you, it was not easy on David to have a bunch of wives. And I know that it hurt Rachel in the beginning, but then Rachel was so gracious. God told Rachel that David was to take another wife. Rachel was cheated out of a lot of things. David used to tell me in the beginning, "Mama, she never had a wedding or a honeymoon. Someday I'm going to give her a real wedding and a real honeymoon." But of course he never got around to it. I know she was very gracious in sharing him. Like I said it was all done very discretely. It wasn't something that was done in front of everyone. I was very close to a lot of those girls.

I wasn't told every time David took a new wife. Sometimes I didn't know until I saw someone was pregnant. I was Mama when it was convenient to be Mama, but otherwise I minded my own business. I didn't walk up to his door and just walk in.

I don't have any ideas about the purpose of what happened in 1993 at Mount Carmel. The message changed at times. Early on, we were taught that we would all walk to Israel dryshod. A lot of Christians believe we are going to be in Israel some day, but David said, you know Israel is not big enough for every Christian in the world to be there. Things change. Clive said David reached more people with his message after he died than before. David always wanted to have a music ministry.

I don't know why that happened the way it did in 1993. I just really admire my son for having the guts to stand up to the United States government for his beliefs. He might not have done everything the way the world thinks he should have, but the Bible tells us not to judge lest you will be judged.

In the world, the men are out there cheating on their wives, most of them have slept with women before they got married, they are doing all of the things they accuse him of doing. The kids, the teenagers, the little girls are going out and sleeping around. David took some wives, but they weren't out in the world sleeping around like they would have been. They were dedicated to David, every one of them. They loved him and he knew that. They understood what they were doing.

I don't understand why God allowed it to happen, why He required it to happen. But just by those things that I saw, I know it had to have been from God. God told Rachel in her dream before David even told her what God had told him to do. I was there. If I had only been told about it, I might not have believed it, but I was there and I saw it.

People talked about why they came to be with David. Take someone like Steve Schneider. He had been an Adventist. He had gone to Adventist schools and was going to be an Adventist preacher. He still had questions. Steve went to a lot of people and questioned them about things. He didn't start getting answers until he started taking studies from David. There were several people who had that experience. Livingstone Fagan is one.[110] Kathy Andrade from California had a lot of questions. She went around asking other people.[111] These were people who had questions[112] and David is the one who answered them.

APPENDIX: POEMS BY DAVID KORESH

Three Napkin Poems by Vernon Howell

Bonnie Haldeman reports that when Vernon Howell was nineteen and going through a difficult emotional period, he would sit in a restaurant and write poems on paper napkins. She possesses three of these "napkin poems," which are transcribed below.

Two of the poems—"Child," and one to which the editor has added the title, "He Sees Beyond the Darkened Skies"—express concerns with identity, time, and apocalypse that prefigure emphases in the life of David Koresh.

"Child" may have been written when Vernon was mourning the loss of his lover, Linda, the mother of his first child, whose father prevented them from marrying.

Following "He Sees Beyond the Darkened Skies" on the same napkin is a bawdy limerick.

The third poem, which the editor has entitled "The Chef's Complaint," consists of the reflections of a young man on boring and thankless work as a short order cook.

"Child"

I once was a child
Full of interest and wonder,
To pretend ment [meant] I could be all.

So my name and world ["woald" or
        "woard"?] change
and my life rearrange,
only then could I stand ten feet tall.

To me there was, yet never was,
One person for me to be.
For how totally could I, then understand
With only one way to see[?]

["]I see[,"] cried the blind man,
["]I hear[,"] cried the deaf,
["]I walk[,"] cried the crip[p]led and lame.

Every body alive, will notice them,
For whole in one they became.

But for me to cry will never help [me]
to be fully content.

For to please those others,
Who with me, share my life,
Another sole [soul] I must present.

So I have become,
Maby [Maybe] one, two, three,
Possibly even four.

If this is to be [. . .]
What ambition have I,
That only to live no more.

[The following verses are on the right side of the napkin, with the right edge torn off.]

So self come for [. . .]
For long you've be[. . .]
In [unclear] complet[. . .].

For love is here
So present yourself [. . .]
That all around may s[. . .].

Wessley Steelbender you [. . .]
A fake. For no love do [. . .]
ever receive.
With open arms, from the [. . .].

[The following verses are in the left hand top corner.]

Who care
The ones who in me believe.
So cry a bit and leave me
now. Never to return again.

For [unclear] room I will lock
With the love I receive
For you steelbender.

The End

Untitled Napkin Poem

[*"He Sees Beyond the Darkened Skies"*]

By Vernon Howell

He sees beyond the darken[e]d skies
and hears the muted bewildered cries
of those devoured by hungard [hungered] flies.
Not living now.

His arms are open[e]d to receive the toll
of those who now have san[c]tioned sole [souls ?]
But few are those ac[c]ording to poll[.]
Not living now.

But menny [many] are them according to tell
Whos[e] fate demanded them only to fail
Whos[e] paths have lead [led] them only to
hell[.]
Not living now.

He sees beyond the darken[e]d skies
For his will be done by the sole [soul] who tries
and for the sole [soul] his will be done denies
Is not living now

Nor Never

_____

For all are not living now you see[,]
For he has not yet his victory
of the battle now present beneith [beneath] the
skies

Between those of truth and those of lies.

He sees beyond the darken[e]d skies
and hear[s] the muted bewildered cries
of those who are known for manny [many] tries
and for those who are known for only lies[.]
He turns his head and simply shys [sighs]
For those not living now.

[The following verses are on the back of the napkin.]

Time you great obsinity [obscenity]
You rob me of my destiny[.]
My does and don[']ts are govern[e]d by you
My love[s,] my hate[s,] the things I do[.]
I must admit[,] Time[,] in the past
Your rule over my mortle [mortal] chast [cast]
Was not a bother[,] no far from[.]
But here [hear] me now[,] Time[,] for love has
come[.]
The prophits [prophets] of old ~~have told~~ of
you[,]
of the wickedness you spame [unclear][,] the
hatred you brewed[.]

But Time y[o]u[']r[e] fucked, for you don[']t see
That even your self has a detiney [destiny],
And along with destiny[,] Time[,] there's fate
So retrace your steps[,] Time[,] before it[']s too
late.

[Below is a separate poem.]

> Oh say can you see
> On my /hush hush/ sleeps a flea
> And by the dawn[']s early light
> I'm sure he will bite[.]

Untitled Poem by Vernon Howell

[*"The Chef's Complaint"*]

1 [The first verses begin half way down.]

Oh great cheff [chef],
Man your station.
To your work in full
you must show dedication.
So cook that egg,
Fry that ham.
Look alive[,] boy,
Or you['ll] answer to Sam.
You work all alone
Maintaining your greel [grill],
Preparing the food,
For your customer[']s fill.
Yet not one thank you,
will you reacieve [receive],
From the customers who
tip the waitress then leave.
And to top it all,
When you[']r[e] dead on your feet[,]
When no more can you move
Do [Due] to the absents [absence] of sleep

[The remainder of the poem is written on the top of the unfolded napkin.]

Then your boss will
Confront you,
and pleading ask[,]
["]Your relieff [relief] cheff [chef] is sick[.]
Do you think you can last[?"]

Then with a [s]neer your hat [unclear, cut off]
Across the room you will [cut off]
Then outloud you cry[,]
["]This job is like hell[!"]

Then one more burger,
you try to fry.
With onion filled eyes,
you begin to cry.

But before you know it,
the day[']s at [an] end.
You go home and sleep,
so you can do it again.

Vernon Howell's Songs on the "Voice of Fire" Audiotape

Clive Doyle reports that the "Voice of Fire" audiotape recorded by Vernon Howell in 1988 or 1989 was directed particularly to Linda, the mother of his first child. In this audiotape, Vernon performs two songs and gives an oration explaining his theology and extending an invitation to join the Branch Davidian community at Mount Carmel and share in their salvation.

The "Voice of Fire" tape begins with a song that has been called "Seven Thunders" on the audiotape (or "The Book of Daniel" on the CD made by the Branch Davidians), warning of the coming apocalyptic events. The song refers to apocalyptic symbols in the books of Daniel and Revelation (especially chap. 10) and also Deuteronomy (God's doctrine "shall drop as the rain" [32:2]). Vernon Howell/David Koresh identified himself with the "mighty angel" (Rev. 10:1) with a rainbow upon his head who is the "seventh angel" (Rev. 10:7), possessing a "little book" (Rev. 10:2), who when he cried out, "seven thunders uttered their voices" (Rev. 10:3). In the song and the following oration Vernon is inviting Linda to join the Branch Davidians so that when God's judgment comes she will be included in God's kingdom.

The audiotape concludes with a song called "Sheshona-him" (spelling on the CD). Dr. James Tabor explains that:

> Shoshanna is the Hebrew for lily, and thus any such flower. It becomes a metaphor for the lips, either the mouth or vulva . . . so it takes on a sexual connotation in the Song of Solomon. It was apparently a "tune" in that several of the Psalms (40, 69, 80) begin with this title: "Set to Shoshan-nim," meaning to that tune on the harp. I think in David's thought it took on a spiritual/metaphorical meaning, but was combined with the "soul mate" idea of souls belonging together. . . .[113]

"Sheshonahim" may refer to the one to whom the Lamb will be married in the "Marriage of the Lamb" (Rev. 19:7-9), which represents salvation in God's kingdom. The "Marriage of the Lamb," discussed by Vernon on the "Voice of Fire" audiotape, is an important part of Branch Davidian theology, and Branch Davidians expect that in God's kingdom the Lamb (Christ) will be married to a woman whose identity is unknown. A portion of "Sheshonahim" can be heard at <http://www.wizardsofaz.com/waco/books.html>.

The lyrics of "Seven Thunders" and "Sheshonahim" represent early works by Vernon Howell/David Koresh after he experienced his calling from God. The audiotape entitled *Songs to Grandpa*[114] also contains early songs with theological content.

"Seven Thunders"
("Book of Daniel")

I've got a secret
That I'd like you to understand.
See the book
There in the angel's hand.
The book of Daniel has got a message,
A message for you, a message for you.

The angel cries
As the lion begins to roar [Rev. 10:3].
Secrets untold,
Mysteries in life to store.
What's the thunder?
Who knows? Don't you understand? Understand?

The book is sealed.
The angel stands on Earth to see.

Don't it make you cry
At all that we can see?
See the cloud,
Feel the rain fall.
Don't you understand, understand?

Seven thunders,
All of Earth a voice.
Now you know,
You've got to make a choice.
Will you listen to the mystery,
the mystery of life? The mystery of life? Ohh.

See the angel
with the book in his hand,
the book of Daniel.
He can teach the eternal plan.
Seven thunders.
Won't you see?
Won't you listen to me?
We've got the key!

In the days of the voice of the Seventh Angel
when he shall begin to sound
the battle has gone before,
going to come to the ground.
The mystery is finished as he hath declared
to his servants the prophets [Rev. 10:7]
Won't you beware? Won't you beware?

Photo 1: Vernon Howell at 6 months old with his cousin at his paternal grandmother's house. Photo courtesy of Bonnie Haldeman.

Photo 2: Vernon Howell, age 2, in Houston. Photo courtesy of Bonnie Haldeman.

*Photo 3: Vernon Howell, at age eight, in Richardson, Texas.
Photo courtesy of Bonnie Haldeman.*

*Photo 4: Vernon Howell and his brother Roger Haldeman at their home
in Richardson, Texas. Photo courtesy of Bonnie Haldeman.*

Photo 5: Roy Haldeman, Bonnie Haldeman, Roger Haldeman, and Vernon Howell. Roger was probably six years old and Vernon was probably twelve. Photo courtesy of Bonnie Haldeman.

Photo 6: Roger Haldeman (probably about six years old) and Vernon Howell (probably about twelve). Photo courtesy of Bonnie Haldeman.

Photo 7: Vernon Howell, about ten years old, dressed up for Easter in the house on Plano Road in Richardson, Texas. Photo courtesy of Bonnie Haldeman.

Photo 8: Bonnie Haldeman, Roger Haldeman, and Vernon Howell. Photo courtesy of Bonnie Haldeman.

Photo 9: Vernon Howell shortly after he left for Mount Carmel in 1981 at age 22. Photo courtesy of Bonnie Haldeman.

Photo 10: Vernon Howell with his maternal grandmother, Erline Clark, and his cousin, Patrick, in 1984 in one of the small houses at Mount Carmel. Bonnie Haldeman along with Erline and Patrick were visiting Vernon. Photo courtesy of Bonnie Haldeman.

Photo 11: Vernon Howell and Rachel Howell as newlyweds in 1984. Photo courtesy of Bonnie Haldeman.

Photo 12: Vernon Howell with his new son, Cyrus Howell, in 1985 at Bonnie and Roy Haldeman's home in Chandler, Texas. Photo courtesy of Bonnie Haldeman.

Photo 13: Vernon Howell with Cyrus Howell.
Photo courtesy of Bonnie Haldeman.

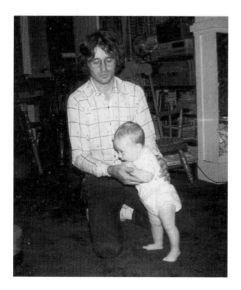

Photo 14: Vernon Howell with Cyrus Howell in California.
Photo courtesy of Bonnie Haldeman.

Photo 15: Brenda Kendrick, Bonnie Haldeman, Karen Doyle,
and Rachel Sylvia (in front) at the Palestine camp in 1985.
Photo courtesy of Bonnie Haldeman.

Photo 16: Michele Jones, Brenda Kendrick, Robyn Bunds, and Karen
Doyle at the Palestine camp in 1986. Photo courtesy of Bonnie
Haldeman.

Photo 17: Stan and Lorraine ("Larry") Sylvia with their children, Joshua and Rachel, at the Palestine camp. Photo courtesy of Bonnie Haldeman.

Photo 18: Rachel Howell with Cyrus Howell at the Palestine camp in 1987. Photo courtesy of Bonnie Haldeman.

Photo 19: Floyd Houtman. Photo courtesy of Clive Doyle.

Photo 20: Clive Doyle at Mount Carmel in 2004. Photo courtesy of
Catherine Wessinger.

Photo 21: Bonnie Haldeman, Vernon Howell (David Koresh), Rachel Howell, and Star Howell at the Cave, a former club in Waco, probably in 1988. Vernon Howell rented the Cave so some Branch Davidians could live there and his band could practice there. Photo courtesy of Bonnie Haldeman.

Photo 22: Vernon Howell (David Koresh) at the Cave. Photo courtesy of Bonnie Haldeman.

Photo 23: *Vernon Howell (David Koresh), Rachel Howell, Cyrus Howell, and Star Howell at the Cave. Photo courtesy of Bonnie Haldeman.*

Photo 24: *Michele Jones at the Cave. Photo courtesy of Bonnie Haldeman.*

Photo 25: Paul Fatta and Sherri Jewell in Hawaii before meeting the Branch Davidians. Photo courtesy of Paul Fatta.

Photo 26: Ness Vaega (who was not a Branch Davidian) with her niece Joann Vaega in front of the Pilica bakery in Hawaii. Photo courtesy of Bonnie Haldeman.

Photo 27: Bonnie Haldeman leaving the apartment behind the bakery in Hawaii. Photo courtesy of Bonnie Haldeman.

Photo 28: Gang at the airport in Hawaii in 1987 to see Greg Summers off on his trip to the mainland. The unidentified man on the far left was not a Branch Davidian. Next is Scott Sonobe, Greg Summers (with lei), Peter Hipsman, looking over the shoulder of Jimmy Riddle, Neil Vaega with Joann Vaega, and Henry and Gertrude Chang. Photo courtesy of Bonnie Haldeman.

Photo 29: Neil and Margarida Vaega on right with Neil holding their daughter Joann. Neil's sister, Ness, is on the left. They are at the airport in Hawaii. Photo courtesy of Bonnie Haldeman.

Photo 30: Judy Schneider, Steve Schneider, and Elizabeth Baranyai at the airport in Hawaii. Photo courtesy of Bonnie Haldeman.

Photo 31: Paul Fatta, Elizabeth Baranyai, and Scott Sonobe at the airport in Hawaii. Photo courtesy of Bonnie Haldeman.

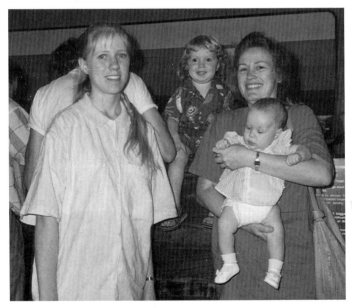

Photo 32: Rachel Howell, Cyrus Howell, Bonnie Haldeman, and Star Howell at the Hawaii airport. Photo courtesy of Bonnie Haldeman.

Photo 33: Vernon Howell (David Koresh), Bonnie Haldeman, and Star Howell at the Hawaii airport. Photo courtesy of Bonnie Haldeman.

Photo 34: A Sabbath afternoon hike in Hawaii. Jimmy Riddle seated on the left with Henry Chang seated behind him. Standing are Joann Vaega, Steve Schneider, Neil Vaega, and Judy Schneider. Judy's dog, Bandito, is on the far left. Photo courtesy of Bonnie Haldeman.

Photo 35: Cutting up in Hawaii. Bonnie Haldeman posing with a stranger's car, and Neil Vaega in the background. Photo courtesy of Bonnie Haldeman.

Photo 36: Mug shot of Vernon Howell (David Koresh) taken after his arrest in 1987 for getting into a shootout with George Roden at Mount Carmel. Photo courtesy of Mount Carmel Visitors' Center.

Photo 37: Nicole Gent and Dayland Lord Gent, her son by Vernon Howell (David Koresh). Photo courtesy of Bonnie Haldeman.

Photo 38: Bonnie Haldeman with Dayland Gent, the son of Nicole Gent and David Koresh. Photo courtesy of Bonnie Haldeman.

Photo 39: Margaret Lawson at Mount Carmel. This photo depicts the
small houses people used to live in at Mount Carmel. Photo courtesy
of Bonnie Haldeman.

Photo 40: Roy Haldeman and Star Howell at Mount Carmel.
Photo courtesy of Bonnie Haldeman.

Photo 41: Tea party at Bonnie Haldeman's house at Mount Carmel with Joshua Sylvia on far left, Cyrus Howell and Star Howell. Photo courtesy of Bonnie Haldeman.

Photo 42: Cyrus and Star Howell in Bonnie Haldeman's house at Mount Carmel. Photo courtesy of Bonnie Haldeman.

Photo 43: Shari Doyle at Bonnie Haldeman's house at Mount Carmel, probably in 1989 or 1990. Photo courtesy of Bonnie Haldeman.

Photo 44: Bonnie Haldeman with Mayanah Schneider, the daughter of Judy Schneider and David Koresh. Photo courtesy of Bonnie Haldeman.

Photo 45: Graduation with a degree in nursing at McLennan
Community College in Waco, Texas, in August 1991.
Photo courtesy of Bonnie Haldeman.

Photo 46: Bonnie Haldeman in front of her house near Chandler, Texas,
in 1993, sometime after the fire at Mount Carmel on April 19.
Photo courtesy of Bonnie Haldeman.

Photo 47: Novellette Sinclair Hipsman on a visit to Bonnie Haldeman's house near Chandler, Texas, in October 1992. Photo courtesy of Bonnie Haldeman.

Photo 48: Star Howell on left, Serenity Sea Jones (daughter of Michele Jones and David Koresh), and Dayland Gent (son of Nicole Gent and David Koresh) in 1993 at Mount Carmel. Photo taken on Bonnie Haldeman's last visit to Mount Carmel in January 1993. Photo courtesy of Bonnie Haldeman.

Photo 49: A photo of Bobbie Lane Koresh, daughter of Rachel Howell, with her father, David Koresh, taken from a video made during the 1993 siege after David Koresh had been wounded in the shootout with the ATF agents. This is Bonnie Haldeman's only photograph of Bobbie Lane. Photo courtesy of Bonnie Haldeman.

Photo 50: Dick DeGuerin, David Koresh's attorney. Photo courtesy of Bonnie Haldeman.

Photo 51: The fire consumes the Mount Carmel residence on April 19, 1993. The Branch Davidians' flag can be seen flying over the building. Government exhibit in the Branch Davidian civil trial.

Photo 52: A firetruck was permitted to spray water after the residence was completely burned down. Government exhibit in the Branch Davidian civil trial.

Photo 53: Karen Doyle, Ron Engelman, Bonnie Haldeman in the crowd at one of the first memorials after the fire. Photo courtesy of Bonnie Haldeman.

Photo 54: Bonnie Haldeman and her mother, Erline Clark, probably in 1994. Photo courtesy of Bonnie Haldeman.

Photo 55: Memorial quilt that was made by Bonnie Haldeman and sent to be displayed in Washington, D.C. Photo courtesy of Bonnie Haldeman.

Photo 56: Bobby Howell (David Koresh's biological father) and his mother, Jean Holub, after a memorial at Mount Carmel in the 1990s. Photo courtesy of Bonnie Haldeman.

Photo 57: Catherine Matteson at Bonnie Haldeman's house in 1994 or 1995. Photo courtesy of Bonnie Haldeman.

Photo 58: Plaque at David Koresh's grave in a cemetery in Tyler, Texas. A vandal had sprayed blue metallic paint on the plaque. Photo courtesy of Catherine Wessinger.

Photo 59: Bonnie Haldeman and Roy Haldeman meeting with scholars visiting Mount Carmel and its rebuilt chapel in 2001. Photo courtesy of Catherine Wessinger.

Photo 60: The chapel built by volunteers on the site of the burned residence was completed in 2000. Earlier crape myrtle trees had been planted for each Branch Davidian who died in 1993. Photo courtesy of Catherine Wessinger.

Photo 61: The crape myrtle trees in bloom in 2003. Photo courtesy of
Catherine Wessinger.

Photo 62: In the courtyard of the Ritz Carlton Hotel on Canal Street in
New Orleans, February 10, 2002. Around the table from the left: Kimberly
Martin (in front), Sheila Martin, Bonnie Haldeman, Gordon Novel (inves-
tigator for the plaintiffs in the civil lawsuit), and Clive Doyle. They were in
New Orleans for a hearing in the Branch Davidians' wrongful death lawsuit
against the government in the United States Fifth Circuit Court of Appeals.
One of the attorneys in the case hosted the Branch Davidians for lunch at
the Ritz Carlton. The Fifth Circuit Court decided against the appeal, thus
effectively ending the case. Photo courtesy of Catherine Wessinger.

Photo 63: From left to right: Kimberly Martin, Sheila Martin, sociologist James T. Richardson, Clive Doyle, Bonnie Haldeman, Catherine Matteson, and Catherine Wessinger at the Cracker Barrel in Waco, Texas, on March 1, 2003. The scholars were in town for the tenth anniversary memorial of the February 28, 1993, ATF raid, held the day before at Mount Carmel. Photo courtesy of Catherine Wessinger.

Photo 64: Bonnie Haldeman with Faith Haldeman, the daughter of Roger Haldeman and Ruth Garney Haldeman, and Buttons in February 2006, in Bonnie's house near Chandler, Texas. Photo courtesy of Catherine Wessinger.

Photo 65: Bonnie Haldeman and Catherine Wessinger in 2001 standing behind the memorial stone listing the names of the Branch Davidians who died in 1993 donated by the Northeast Texas Regional Militia of Texarkana, Texas. In the background can be seen the crape myrtle trees planted for each of the deceased Branch Davidians. Across the street, the house on the left is the "undercover house" used by the ATF agents in 1993. The undercover house was demolished by the owner in 2004. The memorial stone bearing all the names and the smaller memorial stones bearing the names of individual deceased Branch Davidians were moved by Charles Pace to a location near the entrance of the driveway in 2006–2007.
Photo courtesy of Catherine Wessinger.

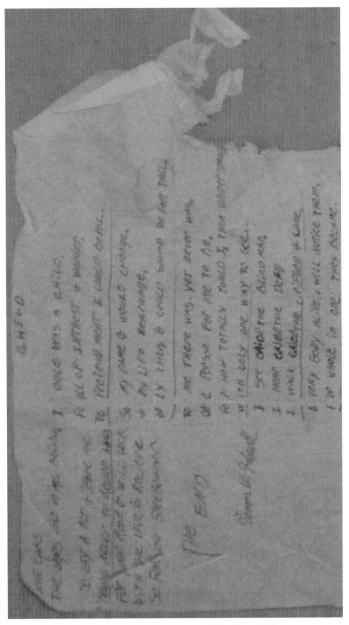

Photo 66: "Child" Poem. Photo courtesy of Catherine Wessinger

A LIFE AS LONG AS I
TO AL TOTALLY FREELY CONTENT YOU ARE

But FOR ME TO SAY WILL NEVER HOL...
BEING TOTALLY FREELY CONTENT

FOR TO PLEASE THOSE OTHERS
WHO WITH ME, STARE MY LIFE,
ANOTHER SIDE I MOST PRESENT

SO WHO HAVE I BECOME,
MANY ONE, I'M TIRED,
FEEBLY AND FAKE

IF THIS IS LIFE,
WITH AMBITION HARD TO
THAN ONLY TO LIVE MY LIFE

He sees beyond the darkend skies
& hears the muted bewildered cries
of those devoured by manmade flies.
Not living now.

His arms are spread to relieve the toll
of those who now have sanctioned sole
but few are those according to roll
not living now

But menny are them according to tell
who fate demanded them only to fail
who's paths have lead them only to hell
not living now

He sees beyond the wooden ——
for His will to be done by the son who ——
& for the sole His will be done dealt
is not living now

Not never

For all are not living now you see
for He has not yet His victory
of the battle now present bewith the soul
between those of truth & those of lies.

He sees beyond the darkend skies
& hear the mad bewildered cries
of those who He knows for many this
for those who are known for only is
He bows His head & simply says.
for those not living now

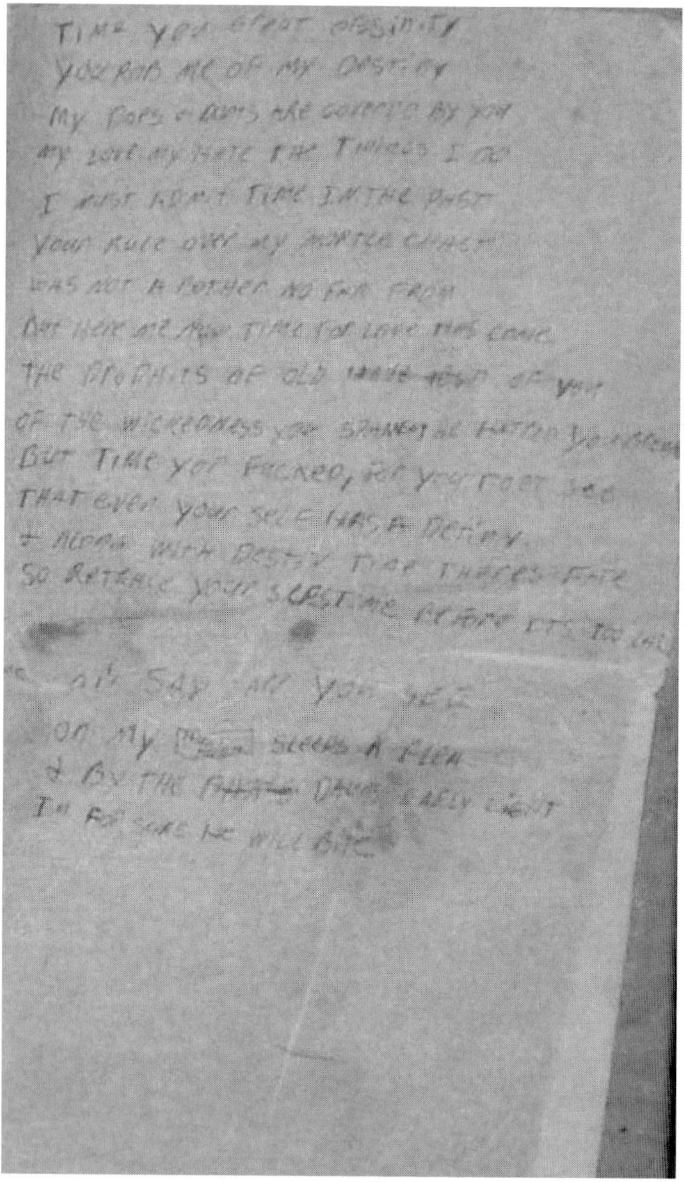

Photo 67: "He Sees Beyond Darkened Skies" Poem. Photo courtesy of Catherine Wessinger.

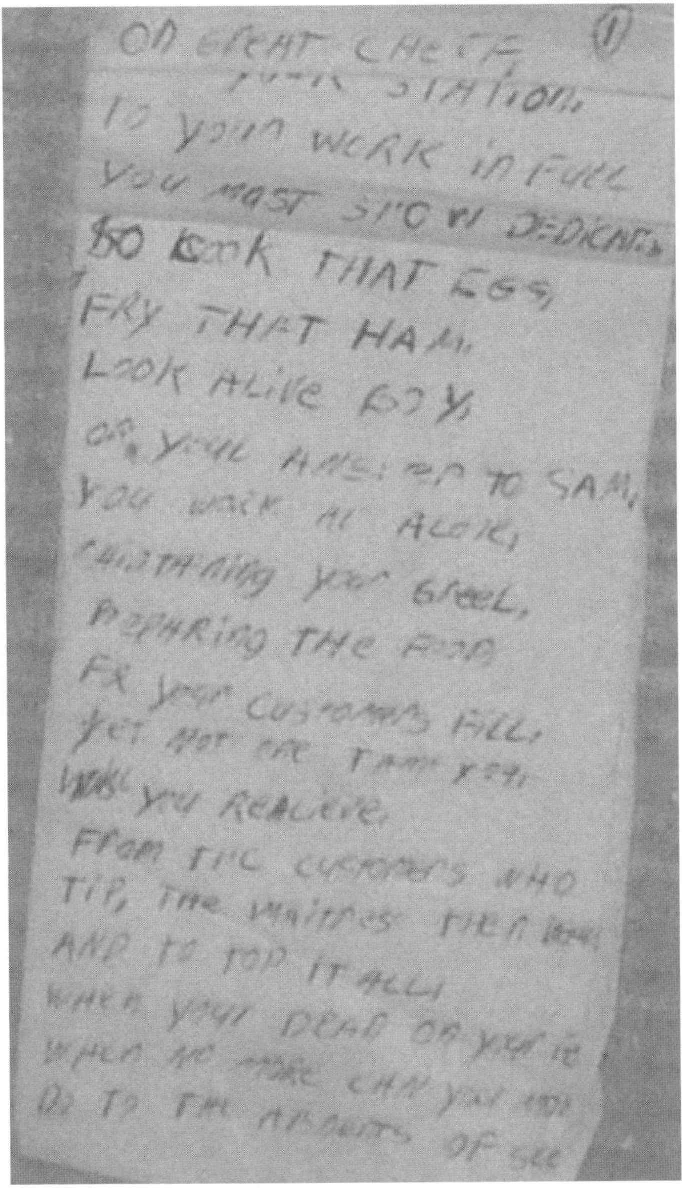

Photo 68: "The Chef's Complaint" Poem. Photo courtesy of Catherine Wessinger.

THEN YOUR BOSS WILL
CONFRONT YOU,
+ PLEADING ASK,

~~[redacted]~~ YOUR REPEAT CHEFF IS SO
DO YOU THINK YOU CAN LAST

THEN YOUR HAT
THEN WITH ANGER YOUR TOSS
ACROSS THE ROOM YOU WILL
~~realize come one ~~ SAY
THIS JOB IS LIKE HELL.

THEN ONE MORE DRIFTER,
YOU TRY TO FRY,
WITH ONION FILLED EYES,
YOU BEGIN TO CRY.

BUT BEFOR YOU KNOW IT,
THE DAYS AT END,
YOU GO HOME + SLEEP,
SO YOU CAN DO IT AGIN.

"Sheshonahim"

Sheshonahim,
She's the only one to see.
Sheshonahim,
She's the only one to hear.
Sheshonahim,
She's the only song to sing.
Sheshonahim,
She's the only one for him.
[Soft lyric that can't be heard.]

I see the sun arising in the morning.
I see the king sitting on the throne.
He's sitting there, sitting all lonely,
Wondering why he has to reign alone.

Sheshonahim,
She's the only one to see.
Sheshonahim,
She's the only one for him.
Sheshonahim,
She's the only one to see.
Sheshonahim,
She's the only one for him.
[Soft lyric that can't be heard.]

I see the sun arising in the morning.
I see the king sitting on the throne.
He's sitting there, wondering why so lonely,
Wondering why he has to reign alone.

Sheshonahim.

David Koresh's Final Poem

On April 19, 1993 Ruth Riddle, who was serving as David Koresh's typist, escaped the fire carrying a floppy disk in her pocket on which was saved David's interpretation of the First Seal of the book of Revelation.

On April 14, 1993 David had sent a letter out to the FBI saying that God had given him permission to write down in "a little book" (Rev. 10:1-2) his interpretations of the apocalyptic symbolism of the Seven Seals discussed in the book of Revelation. David wrote that after the manuscript was given to two Bible scholars, Dr. James Tabor and Dr. Phillip Arnold, for safekeeping, he and the Branch Davidians would come out of the residence. The negotiation transcripts record the Branch Davidians cheering at the prospect of coming out.

This development was in response to the discussion by Dr. Tabor and Dr. Arnold of alternative interpretations of the prophecies of the Bible on a radio program on April 1 to which David and the other Branch Davidians listened. On April 16 David reported to the negotiators that he had completed his interpretation of the First Seal, and the Branch Davidians began requesting wordprocessing equipment to facilitate the completion of the manuscript. The wordprocessing equipment was delivered by the FBI on April 18 at 5:32 p.m., and the typing of the manuscript began immediately.

The FBI tank and CS gas assault began at 6:00 a.m. on April 19.[115]

David Koresh's unfinished manuscript begins with a poem entitled "Eden to Eden," which discusses human perfection lost in the first Eden that is to be regained in God's kingdom, the second Eden. The two love birds appear to be a metaphor for the androgynous human nature that was lost due to sin, which will be restored in God's kingdom. In God's kingdom each person will be given their perfect mate. This understanding of human nature was a Branch Davidian tradition going back to Lois Roden.

The poem refers to Christ's marriage, which occurs in God's kingdom; the Elect are invited to Christ's marriage feast.

"Eden to Eden"

Search forth for the meaning here,
Hidden within these words
'Tis a song that's sung of fallen tears,
Given way for two love birds.

Love birds yet not of feathered creed
Shot down for gambled play,
And caged a far distance betweenst themselves
For the hunter felt it best that way.

"She bird is mine," the hunter said,
'Twas this bird I raised and faithfully fed."
'Twas he bird who released her from her cage,
Sought her womb in youthful age.

Love birds the name, these birds they call,
Two, plural, love bird, takes two.
'Twas not her womb of which he sought,
And certainly not her youth.

Love birds, the name these birds they call,
Two, plural, love bird, takes two,
It's just that he needed she,
To fly the skies of blue.

And now we see the hunter man,
Robbed without a prey,
The evil which he sought to do,
Caused the birds to pass away.

For loneliness and solitaire
Is death to every soul.
For birds of God were meant to pair,
The two to complete the whole.

And now we see the final meaning
Of this rhyme and verse:
The pending judgment of the King
Who rules the universe.

For with Adam and his spirit Eve,
To share the kingdom fair;
But when they sinned they lost their crown
In exchange for shame to bear.

So Eve travailed and brought forth death,
And passed the crown to all;
For each to learn the lesson here,
The kingdom of the fall.

For virgins do not bring forth sons,
Until God does reverse,
The inner meaning of the law,
To remove man from the curse.

For in the Christ we've seen a bride,
The water mixed with blood,

The wife with cloven tongues of fire [Acts 2:3,
    the Holy Spirit],
Of whom the Christ has loved.

And now He's back to sing His song,
The life of every spring,
And love birds gather, each one with mate,
For the marriage of the king.

NOTES

1   Catherine Wessinger, *How the Millennium Comes Violently: From Jonestown to Heaven's Gate* (New York: Seven Bridges Press, 2000), 56–119. The text of this book is available at my website, <http://www.loyno.edu/~wessing>.

2   Mount Carmel Center outside Waco, Texas, was the location of the large residence of the Branch Davidians that was under siege for fifty-one days by FBI agents after a botched Bureau of Alcohol, Tobacco, and Firearms (ATF or BATF) raid on February 28, 1993 that resulted in the deaths of five Branch Davidians and four ATF agents, and wounded on both sides. David Koresh was severely wounded during the shoot-out. Branch Davidian Michael Schroeder was shot and killed by ATF agents later that day. Some Branch Davidians came out during the siege, which ended on April 19, 1993 when FBI agents launched a tank and CS gas assault on the residence that concluded with the great fire that killed seventy-six Branch Davidians including twenty-three children.

3 From the time that Vernon was nineteen, Bonnie begins to refer to him consistently as David. He actually changed his name to David Koresh in 1990 when he was thirty or thirty-one.

4 The memorial on April 19 commemorates the anniversary of the fire at Mount Carmel on April 19, 1993, and all who died at Mount Carmel in 1993.

5 In 1993 Bobby gave an interview about his son, David Koresh, in the book by Kenneth Samples, Erwin de Castro, Richard Abanes, and Robert Lyle entitled *Prophets of the Apocalypse: David Koresh and Other American Messiahs* (Grand Rapids: Baker Books, 1994), 175–76. Concerning David Koresh's participation in the gun trade to support the Branch Davidian community, Bobby Howell reported that David Koresh told him that "he was buyin' the guns and taking them to California and doublin' his money" (176).

6 Bonnie is speaking in 2004.

7 This was a difficult time for Vernon. The children at school called the children in the special class "retarded kids." Vernon dropped out of school in the eleventh grade. Dick J. Reavis, *The Ashes of Waco: An Investigation* (New York: Simon & Schuster, 1995), 25–26.

8 David Thibodeau and Leon W. Whiteson, *A Place Called Waco: A Survivor's Story* (New York: Public Affairs, 1999), 39.

9 These interviews were conducted in this house in Chandler, just outside Tyler, Texas.

10 See <http://www.davidwilkerson.org>, accessed August 7, 2006.

11 Lois Roden, who became the Branch Davidian prophet, had a vision in 1977 that the Holy Spirit was feminine, for which she utilized the Hebrew term *shekinah*. James D. Tabor and Eugene V. Gallagher, *Why Waco? Cults and the Battle for Religious Freedom in America* (Berkeley: University of California Press, 1995), 40. This concept remains important in Branch

Davidian theology. David appears to be asserting here that he had this vision before he met Lois Roden and the Branch Davidians.

12 *Shepherd's Rod* refers to literature distributed by Victor Houteff, the founder of the Davidians, a splinter Seventh-day Adventist group in the 1930s from which the Branch Davidians evolved. The Davidians were also called Shepherd's Rods.

13 Mount Carmel Center is out in the country ten miles east of Waco.

14 Catherine Matteson (77 in 1993) and Margaret Lawson (75) were the first two adults to come out of Mount Carmel after the ATF raid. The came out on March 2 with Daniel (6) and Kimberly (4) Martin bringing an audiotape of David preaching a sermon that David wanted played on primetime television and radio. In return, David promised that they would come out. After the tape was played on KRLD radio and the Christian Broadcasting Network the Branch Davidians prepared to come out, but the David relayed to the FBI that God had told him to wait. Catherine Wessinger, *How the Millennium Comes Violently*, 71. Catherine Matteson was living in Waco in 2006 when she turned 90 in February.

15 In 1991 David Koresh and the Branch Davidians tore down the individual houses at Mount Carmel and used the materials to enlarge the one large residence that became famous in 1993 as the site of the conflict with federal agents and the fire on April 19. The building surrounded a concrete vault that had survived the fire that destroyed the earlier Administration Building, which had burned in 1983. During the CS gas and tank assault carried out by FBI agents on April 19, 1993, the mothers and small children took refuge in the concrete vault and died there. The concrete vault and metal water tower were the only structures left standing after the fire. These were subsequently demolished by the FBI.

16 Rachel was fourteen when they married.

17 Reportedly, David entered into a sexual relationship with Lois Roden in 1983 in an attempt to fulfill Isaiah 8:3 that the prophetess should bear a child. It is on the basis of this alleged relationship that Lois Roden's son, George Roden, made the claim that David had raped Lois. Reavis, *Ashes of Waco*, 75–76; Tabor and Gallagher, *Why Waco?* 41.

George Roden was noted for his erratic and violent behavior. David and about forty of the Branch Davidians left Mount Carmel in 1984 because of George's threats and attacks, including an assault against Catherine Matteson. By that time the core group of Branch Davidians had decided that Lois Roden had lost "her Spirit of prophecy" and that David was the next Branch Davidian prophet. Catherine Matteson, unpublished manuscript, 1994. The information about the transfer of the "Spirit of prophecy" comes from an interview with Catherine Matteson in Waco on October 11, 2004, Matteson Tape #2.

18 Floyd Houtman, African American, was sixty-one, and Novellette Sinclair, African Canadian, was thirty-six, when they died in the fire on April 19, 1993. In 1993 Floyd Houtman's wife and children were no longer part of the Branch Davidian group. Novellette Sinclair was married to Peter Hipsman, European American, to avoid immigration problems.

19 Shari Doyle was eighteen when she died in the fire on April 19, 1993. Her older sister, Karen, was not at Mount Carmel in 1993. Edna Doyle in 1993 was living in a trailer near Mount Carmel looking after some older Branch Davidian women, so she was not involved in the violent events at Mount Carmel. Edna Doyle passed away on July 1, 2001, at eighty-six.

20 David and Robyn Bunds were the children of Donald and Jeannine Bunds who joined the group as a result of David's proselytizing activities in California. Donald and Jeannine purchased a house in California that David and the Branch

Davidians could use. After the Bunds moved to Texas, Robyn became one of David's wives in 1987 when Robyn was seventeen. Eventually Jeannine became one of David's wives also, but she did not bear a child by David. According to David Thibodeau, David Bunds and his wife were expelled from Mount Carmel in 1990 for breaking dietary rules, and they persuaded Robyn to leave taking her son Shaun (called Wisdom). Jeannine Bunds also left the community in 1991. Donald Bunds was living at Mount Carmel in 1993, but had gone out earlier on the day of the ATF raid. Thibodeau and Whiteson, *A Place Called Waco*, 109–10.

Robyn Bunds and David Koresh engaged in a brief dispute for the custody of Shaun and Robyn won. Robyn's statements to federal law enforcement agents about the unconventional sexual arrangements at Mount Carmel heightened their concerns on this subject, although it did not fall within federal jurisdiction. In statements to the media, Robyn depicted herself as a passive, brainwashed follower while at Mount Carmel, although she exercised her autonomy in choosing to leave and take Shaun with her. Jeannine Bunds admitted to the media that when she was at Mount Carmel she entered into a sexual relationship with David Koresh by her own choice. Tabor and Gallagher, *Why Waco?* 119, 122–23, 136–37.

21 David (Vernon) and Rachel went to Israel in January 1985 and returned in February. While there, Vernon had an experience that convinced him that he was the messiah, the Davidic Christ, who would inaugurate and participate in the catastrophic events of the Endtime leading to God's judgment and the creation of God's kingdom. While he was in Jerusalem, Vernon experienced being taken up into heaven and given a scroll to eat. He believed this meant that he was given divine inspiration to interpret and synthesize all of the Bible's prophecies to show how they related to the anticipated Endtime events. Vernon believed that as a result of

this experience he was identified with the Lamb in the book of Revelation and the Seventh Angel in Revelation 10:7. He believed that he had received the "Christ spirit" to be the Endtime messiah. After his return from Israel, Vernon began to teach his interpretations of the biblical prophecies with greater confidence and a sense of authority. James Tabor, "David Koresh and the Branch Davidians," <http://www.pbs.org/wgbh/pages/frontline/shows/apocalypse/explaination/cults.html>, accessed February 6, 2004.

22   Even before Vernon Howell changed his name to David Koresh in 1990, Vernon identified his messianic status with Cyrus (Koresh in Hebrew), the king of the Persians, who liberated the Jews in captivity from the Babylonians in 539 B.C.E. In recognition of Cyrus's great service to the Jews, Isaiah 45:1 calls him a "messiah" ("christ" in Greek translation). [A messiah ("one anointed") in those days in Judaism meant someone who had been anointed by a prophet of God to be the king of the Jews, a priest, or to carry out some other special mission.] Vernon took the first name, David, to indicate his spiritual connection to the Davidic messianic lineage. James D. Tabor, "David Koresh," *Encyclopedia of Religion*, 2d ed. (Detroit: Thomson Gale, 2005), 8:5237–39; Tabor and Gallagher, *Why Waco?* 59–60.

    Vernon understood his experience in Jerusalem as making him the recipient of the "Cyrus message." The ancient King Cyrus had defeated the Babylonians, and the book of Revelation speaks of the fall of "Babylon," a symbol for the corrupt and ungodly social order, in the Endtime events. Tabor and Gallagher, *Why Waco?* 60. It is not clear why Vernon named his eldest son Cyrus.

23   Sheila Martin became a Davidian and then later a Branch Davidian as a young woman living in Boston as a result of meeting a Davidian family, members of which subsequently became Branch Davidians. Raised in the Episcopal Church,

under the Oates family's influence Sheila became a Seventh-day Adventist, but more specifically a Davidian and then later a Branch Davidian Seventh-day Adventist. She met her husband, Wayne Martin, in an Adventist church when she moved to New York City at age twenty-one. They married a year and a half later in 1972. Wayne earned his Master's degree in library science at Columbia University, and his law degree at Harvard. During this time, Wayne tended to fall away from Adventism, while Sheila maintained her commitment to the faith, specifically the Branch Davidian expression of Adventism. The Martin family was living in Durham, North Carolina, where Wayne was assistant professor and law librarian at North Carolina Central University, when in 1982 their fifth child, Jamie, contracted meningitis at age four months. During this traumatic period Wayne .turned back to the Bible and he become interested in David's message as presented on an audiotape Sheila had received. During Jamie's illness, Sheila called Mount Carmel frequently to speak with Lois Roden and also Vernon Howell. She found encouragement from the concern they expressed during this difficult period. In April 1985 Sheila and Wayne and their five children visited the Branch Davidians, then living at the Palestine camp, for Passover. After returning to North Carolina, Wayne quit his job, bought a school bus, and drove his family to join the Branch Davidian community in Palestine. They arrived on May 5, 1985. Catherine Wessinger, "Autobiographies of Three Surviving Branch Davidians: An Initial Report," *Fieldwork in Religion* 1, no. 2 (2005): 165–97.

24 David bought some land in the woods near Palestine, Texas, and the Branch Davidian men cleared out some of the trees and made room for the buses and tents in which people lived.

25 The conference was being held in the Superdome in New Orleans. David went to announce his message to the church.

David was not permitted to get into the conference and speak. Reavis, *Ashes of Waco*, 97–98; Tabor and Gallagher, *Why Waco?* 50–51.

26 Catherine Matteson reported that David returned to Palestine to get his musical instruments and his sound system. He brought them back to New Orleans and set them up on a walkway outside the Superdome where he played for the Seventh-day Adventists while Catherine Matteson and possibly other Branch Davidians handed out literature. Catherine Matteson reported that people would stop and talk with David. Interview with Catherine Matteson in Waco, Texas, on November 26, 2004, Matteson Tape #4.

27 They were probably staying in a house the Branch Davidians had been given in California. David was spending time out in California, doing good works and trying to break into the music scene. Thibodeau and Whiteson, *A Place Called Waco*.

28 The Martins were an African American family from Boston and New York City who had joined the Branch Davidians at the Palestine camp in 1985. Their oldest children were Wayne Joseph Martin, Anita Marie Martin, Lisa Marie Martin, Sheila Renee Martin, and James Desmond Charles (Jamie) Martin, who was severely handicapped due to contracting meningitis when he was four months old. In 1986 Wayne and Sheila Martin left the Palestine camp briefly to return to New York City where Daniel West Martin was born. Their youngest child, Kimberly Renee Martin was born in January 1989 after the Branch Davidians returned to Mount Carmel.

In 1993 Wayne Martin was forty-two, young Wayne Martin was twenty, Anita Martin was eighteen, Lisa Martin was thirteen, Sheila Martin was fifteen when they died in the fire on April 19. During the siege, Jamie (11), Daniel (6), and Kimberly Martin (4) were three of the first four children to be sent out on March 2. Sheila Martin came out on March 21.

Jamie Martin died in 1998. Sheila Martin, forthcoming auto-biography; Wessinger, "Autobiographies of Three Surviving Branch Davidians."

29 Woodrow (Bob) and Janet Kendrick (European Americans) were among the long-time Branch Davidians who transferred their allegiance from Lois Roden to David Koresh.

Their daughter Kathy Kendrick married David Jones, a son of Perry and Mary Belle Jones. The marriage later broke up and Kathy Jones left Mount Carmel, but their children stayed at Mount Carmel with their father.

In 1993 Janet Kendrick was still living at the Palestine camp (see below).

On February 28, 1993, Bob Kendrick (62) and Michael Schroeder (European American, 29) were at an auto repair shop about four miles away from Mount Carmel on Farm Road 2491, which erroneously came to be known in the media as the MagBag. (The MagBag was the name of the business being operated by the Branch Davidians in which the women sewed ammunition vests for sale at gun shows. According to Clive Doyle, the mailing address for the MagBag business was at the auto repair shop, hence the application of the name to the shop by the authorities and the media.) After they heard about the shootout with the ATF agents, Michael Schroeder, Bob Kendrick, and Norman Allison (African British, 28) drove to the Branch Davidians' trailer near Mount Carmel and attempted to return to Mount Carmel on foot. Michael Schroeder was shot and killed by the agents; the agents claimed that he fired at them. Norman Allison was taken into custody. Bob Kendrick escaped back to the trailer where he was arrested on March 9. Bob Kendrick was among the Branch Davidians who were tried in the January 1994 criminal trial, but he was acquitted of all charges along with Norman Allison and Clive Doyle. Reavis, *Ashes of Waco*, 45, 191-99, 278, 298.

30　In 1993 Stan Sylvia (European American) was living with some other Branch Davidians in California. His wife Lorraine ("Larry") was forty when she died in the fire with her two daughters, Rachel (12), fathered by Stan, and Hollywood (1), who was fathered by David Koresh. Reavis, *Ashes of Waco*, 112; List of deceased Branch Davidians compiled by surviving Branch Davidians.

31　While in California, David made an audiotape of some of his songs and sent it to his grandfather while he was in the hospital. David Koresh, *Songs to Grandpa* (Gladewater, Tex.: GMC Records, 1996).

32　The Branch Davidians still don't observe Christmas.

33　James Lawter, European American, was seventy in 1993. No charges were pressed against him. All the Branch Davidians who came out of the residence at Mount Carmel spent time in jail.

34　David was proselytizing in Australia. Clive Doyle had grown up in Australia.

35　James Riddle, European American, was thirty-two when he died on April 19, 1993. He was the brother of Rita Riddle, who came out during the siege. He was married (in name only) to Ruth Ottman Riddle, who escaped the fire. On April 19, 1993 Jimmy Riddle died of a gunshot wound to the head in the back of the Mount Carmel building. The right arm and shoulder blade had been sheared off of his body. When he died, Jimmy Riddle was wearing a jacket with a red lining. David Hardy reports that one of the FBI aerial photographs shown to him by filmmaker Michael McNulty shows a man lying on the ground on a red spot of color with his right arm caught in the tread of one of the tanks. Riddle's autopsy indicated that he suffered no smoke inhalation and had no carbon monoxide in his blood, suggesting that he died before the fire started.

Rick Van Vleet, Stephen M. Novak, Jason Van Vleet, and Michael McNulty, producers, report in the video, "Waco: A New Revelation" (MGA Films, Inc., 1999), that Jimmy Riddle's sister, Rita Riddle arranged for a second autopsy to be performed on Jimmy's skeletal remains. The portion of the skull containing the bullet hole was missing.

FBI agents testified before Congress that no shots had been fired by FBI agents during the CS gas and tank assault on Mount Carmel. Several experts on FLIR (Forward Looking Infrared) photography concluded that flashes on infrared film shot from an airplane flying over Mount Carmel on April 19, 1993 indicated gunfire was directed toward the back of the residence as people were attempting to escape the fire. Tests were conducted at Fort Hood in 2000 as part of the wrongful death civil trial to determine if the flashes on April 19 could have been gunshots. Experts employed by the government concluded that the flashes on the FLIR tapes were too long to have been gunshots and they must have been sunlight reflecting off of debris on the ground. This conclusion continues to be contested by opponents outside the government. The three FLIR experts who were willing to testify that the flashes represented gunshots became severely ill and one died. Within six weeks in 2000, Carlos Ghigliotti (42) died of a heart attack, Dr. Ed Allard suffered a stroke, and Ferdinand Zegel nearly died of blood poisoning apparently caused by an insect bite. See David T. Hardy with Rex Kimball, *This Is Not an Assault: Penetrating the Web of Official Lies Regarding the Waco Incident* (N.p.: Xlibris Corporation, 2001), 44–45, 48–52, 136–40, 148–57, 291. The film by Dan Gifford, William Gazecki, and Michael McNulty, producers, "Waco: The Rules of Engagement" (Los Angeles: Fifth Estate Productions, 1997) depicted Dr. Allard analyzing the FLIR flashes as automatic gunfire directed toward the residence; Michael McNulty carried out his independent FLIR tests in "The F.L.I.R. Project" (Fort Collins, Colo.: COPS Productions, 2001). See John Danforth, Special Council, "Final Report to the Deputy Attorney General Concerning the 1993 Confrontation at the Mt. Carmel Complex, Waco, Texas, November 8, 2000 Pursuant to Order No. 2256-99 of the Attorney General," online at <http://www.apologeticsindex. org/pdf/finalreport.pdf>, for the government's conclusions about the FLIR-captured flashes. See particularly pages 17-29 in the Danforth Report concluding that federal agents did not fire gunshots at the Branch Davidians, and appendices h and i consisting of expert reports on the FLIR evidence.

36 Marc Breault (European American) was from Hawaii and became very close to David Koresh and the keyboard player in David's band. Breault helped David proselytize and recruited his close friends in Hawaii, Steve and Judy Schneider, to the Branch Davidians. Breault and his wife, Elizabeth Baranyai (European Australian), left the Branch Davidians in 1989 when David announced a New Light teaching that all the women in the group, including those married to other men, were David's wives with whom he could propagate children. They became critical of David's sexual relations with under-age girls, and became anticult activists seeking intervention by law enforcement agents. After the fire, Breault published *Inside the Cult* co-authored with Martin King, in which Breault is styled as a "cultbuster." Martin King was with the Australian televison show, *A Current Affair*, when he visited Mount Carmel in 1992 to get footage and interviews for a "cult" story on the Branch Davidians. The slant in the *Current Affair* show, according to King, as with the book co-authored with Breault, was that David Koresh was "a cruel, maniacal, child-molesting, pistol-packing religious zealot who brainwashed

his devotees into believing he was the Messiah, the reincarnation of Jesus Christ, and who would eventually lead them into an all-out war with the United States government and, finally, to their deaths." Tabor and Gallagher, *Why Waco?* 26, 80-93; Marc Breault and Martin King, *Inside the Cult: A Member's Chilling, Exclusive Account of Madness and Depravity in David Koresh's Compound* (New York: Signet Books, 1993). The quotation from Martin King is from p. 12 of this book and is quoted in Tabor and Gallagher, *Why Waco?* 84.

37 David began taking additional young women as his wives in 1986. Many of them were underage, but "married" David with the consent of their parents, who believed that there were biblical reasons for these marriages and the children who would be produced. The first extralegal wife that Bonnie discusses here was fourteen in 1986. David also took Rachel's sister, Michele Jones to be his wife in 1986 when she was twelve. In 1987 David "married" Robyn Bunds (17) and Dana Okimoto (20).

The book of Revelation speaks of the marriage of the Lamb, the Endtime Christ, and David taught that he was that individual. He taught that while Yeshua (Jesus) was perfect and born of a virgin, there were prophecies in the Bible speaking of an imperfect, "sinful" messiah, who would marry and have children. He taught that his children were the "Lord's children" who would be the "twenty-four Elders" discussed in the book of Revelation (4:4 and 5:10) who will participate in the judgment of humanity and help rule God's kingdom.

In 1989 David revealed "New Light" saying that even the married women of the community were his wives, that he was the only male in the community who could propagate children, and therefore all the men should be celibate. Wessinger, *How the Millennium Comes Violently*, 82–84.

David had children with several of the older, married women, such as Judy Schneider (41 in 1993) who died with her daughter, Mayanah (2) in the fire, and Lorraine ("Larry") Sylvia (40 in 1993), who died with her two children, Rachel (12) and Hollywood (1) in the fire.

38 Rachel was twenty-four when she died in the fire on April 19, 1993. Cyrus was eight and Star was six when they died in the fire. Rachel's youngest child, Bobbie Lane, was two when she died in the fire.

39 Bonnie is not identifying this person out of respect for her wishes.

40 Ofelia Santoyo (Mexican American, 62 in 1993) came out of Mount Carmel during the siege in 1993. Her daughter, Julliette Martinez was thirty when she died in the fire, along with her children, Crystal Barrios (3), Isaiah Barrios (4), Joseph Martinez (8), Abigail Martinez (11), and Audrey Martinez (13).

Mary Jean Borst (European American) was forty-nine when she died in the fire. Her son, Brad Borst, left Mount Carmel when he was eighteen. He became a police officer and created a website on the events in 1993 entitled "The Facts about Waco and the Pursuit of Justice," <http://home.comcast.net/~bborst/pursuit_of_justice.html>, accessed January 7, 2006; now defunct.

41 Margarida (Asian New Zealander) and Neil (Samoan American) Vaega, husband and wife, were forty-seven and thirty-eight when they died in the fire. Judy and Steve Schneider (European Americans), husband and wife, were forty-one and forty-three when they died in the fire. Steve Schneider was the person who did most of the negotiating with FBI agents during the 1993 siege. Judy Schneider had a daughter by David Koresh, Mayanah, who was two when she died in the fire. Floracita (Filipina) and Scott (Japanese American) Sonobe, husband and wife, were thirty-four and thirty-five when they died in the fire.

Scott Sonobe was wounded during the shootout with the ATF agents on February 28, 1993 in the hand, wrist, and leg. He may have been one of the Branch Davidians on the second floor who got into a shootout with ATF agents who were attempting to enter through two windows.

Sherri Jewell (European American) was forty-three when she died in the fire. Sherri Jewell's daughter, Kiri, was the subject of a custody battle when her ex-husband was notified by Marc Breault in 1991 that Kiri was going to become one of David Koresh's wives. The court gave custody of Kiri to her father, David Jewell. In 1995 Kiri Jewell testified before a congressional hearing that her mother left her in a motel room with David Koresh when she was ten years old where he had sex with her. The accuracy of Kiri's account is vehemently rejected by the Branch Davidian survivors and Sherri Jewell's mother, Ruth Mosher.

Peter Hipsman (European American) was twenty-eight when he died as a result of the shootout with ATF agents on February 28, 1993. He received serious wounds while he was in David Koresh's bedroom at the top of the four-story central tower. David Thibodeau reports that Hipsman begged to be put out of his misery, so David Koresh sent Neil Vaega to deliver the final shots to the head.

Paul Fatta (35 in 1993, European American) was not at Mount Carmel during the ATF raid on February 28. As the person who funded much of the Branch Davidians' gun trade, Paul Fatta and his son Kalani Fatta (14 in 1993) had left to take stock to a gun show very early that morning. In the 1994 criminal trial Paul Fatta was convicted of arms violations. He was released from prison in 2005.

Tabor and Gallagher, *Why Waco?* 85–86; Thibodeau, *A Place Called Waco*, 169–70, 177–78, 339–40; "Statement of Kiri Jewell, Resident at Mount Carmel, Accompanied by Her

Father David Jewell," in *Activities of Federal Law Enforcement Agencies toward the Branch Davidians: Joint Hearings Before the Subcommittee on Crime of the Committee on the Judiaciary, House of Representatives, and the Subcommittee on National Security, International Affairs, and Criminal Justice of the Committee on Government Reform and Oversight, One Hundred Fourth Congress, First Session, July 19, 20, 21, and 24, 1995,* Part One, Committee on the Judiciary Serial No. 72 (Washington, D.C.: U.S. Government Printing Office, 1996), 147–57; Reavis, *Ashes of Waco,* 296; List of deceased Branch Davidians compiled by surviving Branch Davidians.

42 Shari Doyle was eighteen when she died in the fire. She died of gunshot wounds. Her body was found on top of the concrete vault in which the mothers and small children died, indicating that she was on an upper floor when the building burned down. Interview with Clive Doyle at Mount Carmel on November 27, 2004, Doyle Tape #24; autopsy report for Shari Doyle at <http://www.public-action.com/SkyWriter/WacoMuseum/death/35/35_aut.html>, accessed January 7, 2006. Karen Doyle was not at Mount Carmel in 1993.

43 Greg Summers (European American) was twenty-eight when he died in the fire.

44 Michele Jones (European American) was twelve when David Koresh took her to be one of his wives. She was the daughter of Perry and Mary Belle Jones, and thus the younger sister of David's wife, Rachel. Michele was eighteen when she died in the fire. Her eldest daughter, Serenity Sea Jones was four, and the twins, Chica and Little One, were twenty-two months old, when they died in the fire with their mother. David Koresh was the one who gave the children the creative names. When Michele was sixteen David Koresh asked David Thibodeau to "marry" her (there was no ceremony) to avoid the appearance of his having committed statutory rape and to

tie David Thibodeau into the unconventional Koresh family. Thibodeau and Whiteson, *A Place Called Waco*, 104–5.

45 Peter Gent and Nicole Gent (European Australian), were twins, the children of Bruce and Lisa Gent. They were twenty-four in 1993.

Peter was shot and killed while he was up in the water tower during the ATF raid on February 28. The federal agents alleged that he was up there to shoot at the ATF agents. The Branch Davidians alleged that he was working on the water tower when the raid occurred. The Branch Davidians alleged that he was shot by agents in the helicopters, and the ATF agents denied that they fired any shots from the helicopters. The bullet that killed Peter Gent entered his body in the upper chest and traveled through his body and came to a stop close to his heel, suggesting the shot came from above. After the fire, the metal water tower, which was still standing, was demolished by federal agents and the metal plate containing bullet holes was cut out and removed. The remaining pieces of the water tower are still at Mount Carmel. During the siege, Clive Doyle, Mark Wendel, and Jimmy Riddle retrieved Peter Gent's body from the water tower. He was buried in the front of the building, where tanks ran over the grave. Reavis, *Ashes of Waco*, 133; Thibodeau, *A Place Called Waco*, 227; Clive Doyle while on a tour of the Mount Carmel grounds in December 2005. See the photo of the toppled water tower with the top portion cut out in J. J. Robertson, *Beyond the Flames: This Is the True Story of the Massacre at Waco* (San Diego: J. J. Robertson, 1996), 284.

Nicole Gent became one of David Koresh's wives in Australia in 1988 when she was nineteen. She had a "cover marriage" to Jeff Little (European American), who was thirty-two when he died in the fire. Nicole died with her children, Dayland (3) and Paige (1), in the fire as they huddled in the concrete room. Nicole was four months pregnant. Nicole died from a gunshot wound to the head. Thibodeau, *A Place Called Waco*, 69, 104, 109; Reavis, *Ashes of Waco*, 277; Autopsy of Nicole Gent Little, at <http://www.public-action.com/SkyWriter/WacoMuseum/death/47/47_aut.html>, accessed January 7, 2006.

The other pregnant mother was Aïsha Gyarfas Summers (European Australian), who was seventeen when she died with her daughter Startle Summers (1). Aisha's "cover husband" was Greg Summers (European American, 28 in 1993). Aisha's autopsy report states that she died of a gunshot wound to the left chest and from asphyxiation from inhalation of smoke and carbon monoxide. The baby was near-term. Autopsy of Aisha Summers at <http://www.public-action.com/SkyWriter/WacoMuseum/death/31a/31a_aut.html>. and of "Fetus Summers," at <http://www.public-action.com/SkyWriter/WacoMuseum/death/31b/31b_aut.html>, accessed January 7, 2006.

46 Ben Roden (1902–1978) was the founder of the Branch Davidians as they split off from the Davidians in 1959. Ben Roden, the husband of Lois Roden and father of George Roden, was the prophet immediately preceding Lois. The Rodens saw themselves in the prophetic lineage of Ellen G. White (1827–1915), the prophet of the Seventh-day Adventist Church, and Victor Houteff, the founder of the Davidians established in Waco in 1935. Lois Roden died in 1986 while the Koresh Branch Davidians were living at the Palestine camp.

47 When David Thibodeau attended the November 1993 meeting of the American Academy of Religion in Washington, D.C., he confirmed that the members of the group did not call themselves Branch Davidians. They considered themselves to be students of the Bible. They also considered themselves to be members of the large Koresh family.

48 A Receivers Deed dated February 27, 1973 says that the prop-
    erty at Mount Carmel was purchased by Benjamin Roden,
    Lois Roden, and George Roden, Trustees for the General
    Association of Branch Davidian Seventh Day Adventists.
    This is where reporters got the name "Branch Davidians" in
    1993 when they were seeking to determine the identity of the
    group.

49 Clive Doyle was present at this interview with Bonnie on July
    2, 2004, at Bonnie's house in Chandler, Texas, Haldeman
    Tape #3. At this point, Bonnie asked him to fill in the story
    of David's shootout with George Roden. The following is
    Clive Doyle's account integrated into Bonnie's narrative.

50 The sheriff's deputies appear not to want to get involved.

51 Amo Paul Bishop Roden claimed to be George Roden's
    common law wife and that she had a child by him. On the
    basis of her claim of this relationship and membership in the
    Roden group of Branch Davidians, she asserted her right to
    ownership of the Mount Carmel property shortly after the
    fire. She lived on the property in a shack for some time. Amo
    was living at Mount Carmel when Clive Doyle moved onto
    the property in February 1999. Amo moved away after a jury
    in 2000 decided that none of the claimants were trustees of
    the General Association of Branch Davidian Seventh-day
    Adventists. Doyle Tape #22, interview with Clive Doyle on
    November 27, 2004 at Mount Carmel; Letter from Clive
    Doyle dated December 10, 2004; "Judgment" in *Trustees of
    the Branch Davidian Seventh-day Adventists Association v. George
    Buchanan Roden and Amo Bishop Roden et al.*, District Court
    of McLennan County, Texas, 74th Judicial District, No. 96-
    1152-3.

    When Catherine Wessinger visited the property in 2004
    Amo Roden was camped by the front gate living out of her
    truck. Any visitor coming to Mount Carmel encountered

Amo Roden first. She told visitors that she was the true representative of the Branch Davidians and not a "Koreshite," and that Clive Doyle, living in his trailer on the property, was not a Branch Davidian. She solicited donations for her literature.

In 2004 Amo filed a request for a restraining order against Clive Doyle and the McLennan County Sheriff's Department and threatened other legal proceedings to gain ownership of the property. She was practicing *pro se* litigation by drawing up her own legal documents. In 2005, after Charles Pace, who also lived on the property, towed her truck off for the second time, and after a hearing in court with Bill Johnston, the former federal prosecutor in the 1994 Branch Davidian criminal trial, representing Charles Pace and Clive Doyle, Amo Roden ceased attempting to squat on the property. When Catherine Wessinger visited in December 2005, Amo was bicycling down to Mount Carmel on Saturdays and Sundays to stand on the road next to the gate to solicit donations from visitors who came by for her literature.

"Original Petition and Complaint," *Amo Paul Bishop Roden v. Clive Doyle and the McLennan County Sheriff's Department*, District Court of McLennan County, Texas, 74th Judicial District, No. 2004-3493-3; personal communications from Clive Doyle; March 2005 Newsletter mailed out by Clive Doyle for the General Association of the Branch Davidian Seventh-day Adventists. *The Lights and Shadows of Waco: Millennialism Today* by James Faubion (Princeton: Princeton University Press, 2001) is about Amo Paul Bishop Roden and her theology.

52 Clive's section ends here and Bonnie picks up the story.

53 David and Paul Fatta paid $5,000 each in bail. David Jones also paid $5,000 in bail so he could go back to work to support his family. Reavis, *Ashes of Waco*, 79.

54 After this point, Clive picks up the story again. Bonnie was not present for the initial return to Mount Carmel, so the

pronouns have been changed to reflect the fact that she was not there. Clive Doyle was present when the group reclaimed Mount Carmel.

55 When George was released from jail, he moved to Odessa, Texas, his parents' hometown. He killed a man in 1989 and was thereafter confined to a mental hospital. George Roden died in 1998 at age sixty from a heart attack on the grounds of the Big Spring State Hospital. Reavis, *Ashes of Waco*, 82; Wessinger, *How the Millennium Comes Violently*, 117 n. 130.

56 When the Branch Davidians returned to Mount Carmel, David paid the property taxes that had not been paid for the previous nineteen years, which amounted to $62,000. Reavis, *Ashes of Waco*, 81.

57 Clive is continuing the account.

58 Bonnie resumes her narrative.

59 The trial, held in April 1988, lasted for ten days. The seven men accompanying David Koresh were acquitted of attempted murder. The jury could not come to a decision about Koresh, so he was released. Reavis, *Ashes of Waco*, 79–81.

60 Clive continues here. Pronouns have been changed to match Bonnie's voice and experiences.

61 Bonnie picks up her narrative.

62 From this point Clive adds the following information.

63 The affidavit written by ATF agent Davy Aguilera to obtain the search and arrest warrants that the ATF agents were attempting to deliver on February 28, 1993 alleged that the Branch Davidians were operating a methamphetamine lab. It is illegal in the United States to utilize military equipment and personnel against civilians. Exceptions are made when a "drug nexus" is alleged. The 1996 House of Representatives majority report concluded that the allegation of a methamphetamine lab at Mount Carmel was a lie knowingly told by ATF agents to gain military assistance in the form of surveillance overflights by the National Guard, the use of National

Guard helicopters during the ATF raid, and military assault training by Army Special Forces at Fort Hood prior to the raid. The allegation of a drug nexus was also used to justify the military equipment (operated by FBI agents) and support military personnel during the siege and the assault on April 19, 1993. Wessinger, *How the Millennium Comes Violently*, 63–64; House of Representatives, *Investigation into the Activities of Federal Law Enforcement Agencies Toward the Branch Davidians: Thirteenth Report by the Committee on Government Reform and Oversight Prepared in Conjunction with the Committee on the Judiciary together with Additional and Dissenting Views* (Washington, D.C.: U.S. Government Printing Office, 1996), 30–55.

64 Bonnie's account resumes.

65 Dana Okimoto is a Japanese American woman that David met in Hawaii. The book by Samples, de Castro, Abanes, and Lyle entitled *Prophets of the Apocalypse*, 182–89, contains a 1993 interview with a former Koresh wife given the pseudonym of Diana Ishikawa. She described how David wooed her and persuaded her to become one of his wives when she was twenty years old. She was living with the Branch Davidians and her two sons in California and David was at Mount Carmel, when she decided to call her uncle, who was nearby, to ask him to pick them up. Shortly after that she took her sons with her to Hawaii. Dana Okimoto's two sons, called Sky and Scooter in the Branch Davidian community, are among the four surviving children of David Koresh. The other two surviving children are Shaun, the son of Robyn Bunds, and Shae, the daughter born to Linda before David joined the Branch Davidians. Dana Okimoto appeared in the television report for *Primetime: Witness* entitled *The Children of Waco*, Jude Dratt and Jennifer Lew Goldstone, producers, broadcast April 17, 2003 (New York: ABC News).

66 Graeme Craddock (European Australian, 31 in 1993) was an electrical engineer and a physics high school teacher in Australia. After visiting Mount Carmel several times he moved

to Mount Carmel in March 1992 after being invited to come by Steve Schneider who said that it appeared that prophecies of preliminary Endtime events would soon be fulfilled. By March 1992 the incidents that led Steve to conclude that their community might be attacked soon included an investigation by Child Protective Services into the treatment of the children at Mount Carmel and signs that suggested that the Branch Davidians might be under surveillance by law enforcement agents. Graeme Craddock survived the fire by exiting the building and taking cover in a small cinder block structure. In the 1994 criminal trial, Graeme Craddock was convicted of arms violations based on his own testimony that he possessed weapons during the ATF raid. He was released from prison in 2006 and deported to Australia. Oral and Videotaped Deposition of Graeme Craddock, October 28, 1999, *Isabel G. Andrade, et al v. Phillip J. Cojnacki et al.*, United States District Court for the Western District of Texas, Waco Division, No. W-96-CA-139, 1:205, 2:343; Reavis, *Ashes of Waco*, 183–85, 296, 299; Thibodeau and Whiteson, *Ashes of Waco*, 123; personal communication from Clive Doyle.

67   Janet McBean (25 in 1993, African British) was not at Mount Carmel in 1993 when the ATF raid, the siege, and fire occurred. John-Mark McBean (African British, 27 in 1993) died in the fire.

68   Roger Haldeman was not living at Mount Carmel when Bonnie and Roy left. He returned to Mount Carmel later, and left two weeks before the ATF raid.

69   The house has a front yard and a large field in the back totaling six acres.

70   Bonnie is speaking in July 2004.

71   The date of the fire.

72   Generally, the first floor was reserved for the men's rooms. The women with children had rooms on the second floor. The women without children had rooms on the third floor

of the east and west towers. David's room appears to have been moved around the upstairs area. He had a room on the second floor behind the stairway. He also had a room in the four-story central tower. Doyle Tape #22, recorded on November 27, 2004, at Mount Carmel Center; Telephone interview with Clive Doyle on February 6, 2005; Interview with Catherine Matteson on November 26, 2004 in Waco, Matteson Tape #3.

73 Lisa Farris (European American) was twenty-four when she died in the fire.

74 Diana Henry (African British) was twenty-eight when she died in the fire.

75 Mount Carmel was under surveillance by this time by the ATF and other federal agencies. ATF agents, claiming to be students, had moved into one of the houses across the street on Double E Ranch Road. The Branch Davidians recognized immediately that they were not students. The ATF had requested surveillance overflights also.

76 ATF agent Robert Rodriguez was known to the Branch Davidians at that time as Robert Gonzalez. He was the agent stationed in the undercover house across the street who visited Mount Carmel most often. Rodriguez's assignment was to go inside the Branch Davidians' residence and scout for weapons. He visited David Koresh numerous times at Mount Carmel and David gave him Bible studies and invited him to move to Mount Carmel, although David was quite aware that Robert was probably an undercover agent for a federal agency. David was also aware that his gun-buying activities were under investigation by the ATF and through his gun dealer he invited the ATF agents to come to Mount Carmel openly and inspect his weapons. The agents living across the street even came over to Mount Carmel to shoot guns with David behind the Mount Carmel residence. Robert Rodriguez reported that he saw no illegal weapons at Mount Carmel. Therefore, in order to obtain the warrant to carry out

the raid, the ATF affidavit alleged that the Branch Davidians were a "cult" and that David Koresh was abusing the children, an allegation that had been investigated by Texas Child Protective Services, which had closed the case due to lack of evidence.

Robert Rodriguez was inside the Mount Carmel residence with David Koresh on the morning of February 28, 1993 when David Koresh was informed that a raid was imminent. David told Rodriguez that he knew the agents were coming and he wished Robert good luck. Rodriguez left hurriedly driving his truck down the driveway with the car siren on and beeping his horn. He rushed into the undercover house and called his commanders to tell them that the element of surprise had been lost. He begged them to call off the raid, but instead the commanders told the ATF agents to hurry up and get inside the cattle trailers that would convey them to Mount Carmel to carry out the raid. Wessinger, *How the Millennium Comes Violently*, 60–65, 97–98; "Statement of Robert Rodriguez, Special Agent, Bureau of Alcohol, Tobacco, and Firearms," in House of Representatives, *Activities of Federal Law Enforcement Agencies*, 1:749-55; Sheila Martin Tape #2B, interview recorded on October 10, 2004 in Fort Worth, Texas.

77 They were making ammunition vests. The business was called MagBag. Its mailing address was at a car repair shop down the road from Mount Carmel that the Branch Davidians operated. The press subsequently and erroneously dubbed the car repair shop the MagBag. Personal communication from Clive Doyle.

78 Alerted by the complaints of Marc Breault and other former Branch Davidians about David's sexual activities with underage girls and his acquisition of guns, *Waco Tribune-Herald* reporters Mark England and Darlene McCormick had been researching the Branch Davidians for the previous year with the intention of publishing an exposé. During their

investigation they kept bumping into ATF agents who were also investigating the Branch Davidians. The *Waco Tribune-Herald* editors were trying to publish their "Sinful Messiah" series before the raid, and the ATF agents wanted to carry out the raid before the series came out, thinking that the series could motivate heightened defensive preparations at Mount Carmel. The *Waco Tribune-Herald* published the first installment of the series on Saturday, February 27, because the editors had heard that the ATF would carry out the raid on Monday, March 1. With the publication of this story, the ATF commanders moved the raid up to Sunday, February 28. *Waco Tribune-Herald* reporters heard that the raid would occur on Sunday, so three carloads of newspaper reporters and a couple of cars carrying reporters and cameramen with KWTX-TV were cruising the roads around Mount Carmel early in the morning with the reporters hoping to get into good vantage points to cover the raid. The presence of the reporters and cameramen alerted the Branch Davidians to the impending raid.

The second installment of the "Sinful Messiah" series was published in the *Waco Tribune-Herald* on the morning of February 28. After the raid, the rest of the articles were published in the following day's newspaper. The series, which painted David Koresh as a "cult leader" and the Branch Davidians as a "cult," was the first reference for the hordes of reporters that then descended on the Waco and Mount Carmel areas. Catherine Wessinger, "The Branch Davidians and Religion Reporting: A Ten-Year Retrospective," in *Expecting the End: Millennialism in Social and Historical Context*, ed. Kenneth G. C. Newport and Crawford Gribben (Waco: Baylor University Press, 2006), 147–72, 270–74.

79 The raid was carried out by seventy-six ATF agents at 9:45 a.m. on Sunday morning, February 28, 1993. Three National Guard helicopters flew in from behind the residence carrying ATF agents. Cattle trailers loaded with ATF agents wheeled

up to the front door of the building and agents jumped out. Some approached the front door, and two other teams ran to the right and left sides of the building to climb on the roof and attempt to enter a room in the central tower. The agents were intending to carry out a no-knock "dynamic entry," despite the fact that the search warrant did not authorize such a raid. David Koresh, unarmed, met the agents at the door, with his father-in-law, Perry Jones, standing behind him. There were probably armed men standing behind David and Perry. It is disputed which side shot first.

Attorney David Hardy, who filed numerous Freedom of Information requests and lawsuits to obtain records relating to the case, points out that the amount of evidence in the possession of ATF agents that turned up missing or destroyed raises suspicions about how the shooting started. The ATF had three video cameras operating in the front of the building, including one videotaping from the undercover house across the street, a still camera on a tripod, and a still camera being operated by Public Information Officer Sharon Wheeler. After the raid, Wheeler's camera disappeared from a table in a room filled with ATF agents. It was claimed that the other cameras malfunctioned. See Hardy and Kimball, *This Is not an Assault*, 187, 196.

The Branch Davidians in the front of the building later speculated that the first shots may have been fired by agents killing dogs in a pen at the front door. Some Branch Davidians in the back of the residence, including Renos Avraam and Catherine Matteson, reported that they saw gunfire coming from the three helicopters that were flying toward the Mount Carmel residence on a diagonal line from the northwest. The ATF agents denied that any shots were fired from the helicopters. Two videotapes shot from the helicopters have been obtained by David Hardy and Michael McNulty, researcher for three movies about the 1993 events at Mount Carmel. Both videotapes have had portions deleted at exactly the same moments in the raid. Hardy concludes that the gunshots heard on one videotape must have been fired from the helicopter; gunshots coming from Mount Carmel could not have been heard because of the noise of the helicopter. However, two thumps can be heard in the videotape, and Hardy believes these were the sounds made by bullets fired from Mount Carmel hitting the helicopter. Photographs of the bullet holes in the helicopter's side were made after the raid. Hardy concludes that the shooting began in the back of the building, was heard by the Branch Davidians and agents on the front of the building, who then began exchanging gunfire. Hardy points out that landmarks on the ground revealed in the videotapes indicate that the helicopters came within about one hundred yards of the building rather than the three hundred and fifty yards reported by the pilots.

Hardy interviewed Jim Freeman, a neighbor of the Branch Davidians, whose house was north of Mount Carmel. He was standing in his yard when he saw the helicopters flying at a low altitude toward Mount Carmel. Freeman reported that he heard six or eight initial shots flying through the air either coming from the helicopters or from the ground. When the general shootout began, Freeman could hear a clear distinction between the sounds of the shots fired at the front of the building and those fired either toward or from the helicopters in the back of the building.

Hardy theorizes that since the helicopters were arriving later than planned, agents in the helicopters felt that the agents in the front of the building needed some assistance and therefore fired shots. The raid leader, Philip Chojnacki, was in one of the helicopters. Chojnacki was the commander who ordered the raid to proceed even though Robert Rodriguez had informed him that the element of surprise had been lost. See Hardy and Kimball, *This Is Not an Assault*, 24, 188–96.

After the shootout was over and the ATF agents had pulled back, David Koresh and Steve Schneider were on the telephone with ATF agent Jim Cavanaugh, the deputy raid coordinator stationed in the undercover house across the street. Cavanaugh was serving as negotiator until FBI agents arrived. David asked Steve to ask Jim about the "fire from the helicopters, how it shot my room up, more than any other room. . . ." Jim Cavanaugh denied that the helicopters had guns. At that point David became infuriated, "That's a lie. That is a lie. He's a damn liar," and got on the phone himself. The negotiation transcript reports David as saying:

David: These lies are not making you look very good to anybody here. Now, didn't you say that the helicopters had guns but they didn't fire? Well, you are wrong. You are dead wrong. That may be what you want the media to believe, you know, but there's other people who saw, too. Now tell me, Jim, again. You're honestly going to say those helicopters didn't fire on any of us?

Jim Cavanaugh went on to qualify his statement:

Jim: Okay, what I'm saying is that those helicopters did not have *mounted guns*, okay?

A little later Jim Cavanaugh elaborated on his assertion:

Jim: Okay. What I'm saying is, *I'm not disputing the fact that there might have been fire from the helicopters.* If you say there was fire from the helicopters and you were there, that's okay with me. What I'm telling you is, there was no mounted guns, you know, outside mounted guns on those helicopters.

David: I agree with you on that.

Jim: All right, then that's, that's the only thing I'm saying. Now the agents on those helicopters had guns.

Hardy and Kimball, *This Is Not an Assault*, 25, 190–91; italics added by Hardy. To listen to this exchange between David Koresh and Jim Cavanaugh view "Waco: The Rules of Engagement."

Concerning the events at the front of the building, the Branch Davidians reported that David stood at the front door to meet the agents and said words to the effect of "There's women and children in here. Let's talk." Once the shooting began, David took cover inside and the doors were shut. The ATF agents and armed Branch Davidian men shot at each other through the metal double doors. The Branch Davidians alleged that the bullet holes in the doors would have proved that the ATF agents did most of the shooting. They alleged that most of the bullet holes on the right side of the door were fired from the outside. The right-hand door disappeared after the fire. Only the left-hand door was produced for evidence.

According to the Branch Davidians, Perry Jones was severely wounded in the abdomen and began screaming in pain and begging to be permitted to kill himself. Branch Davidian Kathy Schroeder (European American, 34 in 1993, and wife of Michael Schroeder) testified for the criminal trial that David gave Neil Vaega permission to shoot Perry to put him out of his misery. Perry died of a bullet wound to the mouth. The Tarrant County medical examiner's report did not mention a wound in Perry Jones' abdomen, but the body could not be reexamined because somehow the refrigerator containing some of the Branch Davidian bodies, including Perry's, stopped functioning.

While the shootout was going on at the front door, two teams of ATF agents tried to enter through two windows on the second floor. There was a shootout in this area as well, possibly involving Scott Sonobe.

In the entire shootout, four ATF agents were killed: Todd McKeehan (28), Conway LeBleu (36), Robert Williams (27), Steve Willis (32), all European Americans. Many agents were wounded, some very seriously. Five Branch Davidians died as a result of the shootout: Winston Blake (African British, 28), Peter Gent (European Australian, 24), Peter Hipsman (European American, 28), Perry Jones (European American, 64), and Jaydean Wendel (European American, 34). Michael Schroeder (European American, 29) was shot and killed later in the day as he attempted to walk back to Mount Carmel. The bullets were coming through the walls of the residence. Several Branch Davidians sustained wounds of varying degrees of severity: David Jones (European American, 38) had a bullet stopped by his tailbone, Scott Sonobe was struck by a bullet that went through his left hand and hit his leg, Judy Schneider had a bullet go through her forefinger and shoulder. David Koresh sustained a serious wound to his side as well as a wound to his wrist.

As soon as the shooting started, Wayne Martin and David Koresh both dialed 9-1-1 and begged for the shooting to stop. Wessinger, *How the Millennium Comes Violently*, 56–68; Branch Davidian 9-1-1 audiotapes, February 28, 1993; Thibodeau and Whiteson, *A Place Called Waco*, 170, on Sonobe; Autopsy of Perry Dale Jones, at <http://www.public-action.com/SkyWriter/WacoMuseum/death/80/80_aut.html>, accessed January 7, 2006.

In her deposition for the civil trial, Kathy Schroeder was extremely vague about the matter of someone shooting

Perry Jones and also Peter Hipsman to put them out of their misery. She did not seem to be sure if it was Greg Summers or Neil Vaega, and gave no indication that she witnessed these events herself. She also misplaced the location of Perry's death, putting it at the front door. "Oral Deposition of Kathryn Schroeder, August 30, 1999," *Isabel G. Andrade, et al v. Phillip J. Chojnacki et al.*, and United States of America, United States District Court, Western District of Texas, Waco Division, Civil Action No. W 96 CA 139: 139, 195.

The ATF raid was completely unnecessary. David had a history of cooperating with law enforcement agents, as the earlier episode involving the shootout with George Roden demonstrated. Through his gun dealer David had extended an invitation to ATF agents to inspect his weapons. The ATF undercover agents who had been inside Mount Carmel reported seeing no illegal weapons. David's sexual activities with young girls did not come under ATF jurisdiction. Despite allegations made by ATF commanders that David never left Mount Carmel, he often left and in fact had ATF agents Robert Rodriguez and Jeffrey Brzozowski over to Mount Carmel to shoot guns in the back of the residence. Rodriguez and Brzozowski brought over AR-15 rifles and David supplied some ammunition. There was ample opportunity to arrest David peacefully.

In 1993 the ATF was an embattled agency, having a reputation for breaking into citizen's homes ("dynamic entries"), grossly discriminating against African American agents, and condoning sexual assaults on its female agents. The first Bill Clinton administration was newly arrived in Washington. The ATF probably hoped to get some good publicity over "taking out" a "cult" to make a favorable impression for an upcoming appropriations hearing in Washington and to prevent the Clinton administration from deciding to shut it down. The ATF had made numerous preparations to photograph and videotape the raid, but mysteriously after the raid those cameras appeared to have malfunctioned or were stolen, and the surviving videotapes had portions erased. We have images of the raid only from the KWTX-TV cameraman who followed the cattle trailers carrying the agents into the property and got pinned down by gunfire at the front of the building. See Hardy and Kimball, *This Is not an Assault*, 173–84; Wessinger, "The Branch Davidians and Religion Reporting."

80 David said, "Hello Mama. It's your boy. They shot me and I'm dying, alright? But I'll be back real soon, okay? I'm sorry you didn't learn the Seals, but I'll be merciful, okay? I'll see ya'll in the skies." Reavis, *Ashes of Waco*, 24.

The "Seals" here were a reference to the Seven Seals in the book of Revelation, which were central to David's apocalyptic message about the Endtime events. Only the "Lamb" had the ability to "open" or interpret the Seven Seals. Since David convincingly interpreted the prophecies in the Bible and thus was regarded as having "opened" the Seals, David was seen as the Lamb or the apocalyptic messiah (Christ) by the Branch Davidians. David had predicted that he would be killed by the agents of evil "Babylon." "Babylon" in the book of Revelation represents the social order and government that is aligned with Satan.

David's message left for Bonnie indicated that he believed he was dying from the wounds sustained in the shootout in fulfillment of that prophecy. David believed that after his death he would be resurrected to lead God's army, defeat evil, and then as the Endtime Christ, judge everyone so that God's kingdom would be created. Tabor and Gallagher, *Why Waco?* 54, 76–79; David Koresh, KRLD interview audiotape, April 19, 1993; David Koresh, March 2, 1993 audiotape.

81 Dick DeGuerin is a famous criminal attorney in Texas. He agreed to represent David Koresh.

82 Bellmead is the town just north of Waco that is very convenient to Mount Carmel.

83 After the botched ATF raid on February 28, FBI agents arrived to take over the siege. Studies of the negotiation transcripts have demonstrated that the majority of the Branch Davidians were not going to come out unless they understood the scenario as conforming to God's will as given in the Bible's prophecies. The FBI negotiators were instructed by the on-site commander, Special Agent in Charge Jeffrey Jamar, not to listen to their "Bible babble," thus the FBI agents ignored the religious dimension that was most important to the Branch Davidians. On the negotiations see Jayne Seminare Docherty, *Learning the Lessons from Waco: When the Parties Bring Their Gods to the Negotiation Table* (Syracuse: Syracuse University Press, 2001).

Eugene V. Gallagher has stressed that David's interpretations of the biblical prophecies were not set in stone. They were constantly being adjusted in response to the events. See Eugene V. Gallagher, "'Theology Is Life and Death': David Koresh on Violence, Persecution, and the Millennium," in *Millennialism, Persecution, and Violence: Historical Cases*, ed. Catherine Wessinger (Syracuse: Syracuse University Press, 2000), 82–100.

An interpretive log of the siege events compiled by James Tabor demonstrates that every time Branch Davidian adults came out, the FBI punished them by increasing the psychological warfare that was waged against them. The Branch Davidians were surrounded by tanks that made menacing maneuvers and the drivers made threatening remarks and insulting gestures. The Branch Davidians' electricity was cut off, they were blasted by high decibel irritating sounds, and had bright spotlights shone at them throughout the nights. James Tabor, "The Events at Waco: An Interpretative Log," http://home.maine.rr.com/waco/ww.html, now defunct; the interpretive log is currently located at http://ccat.sas.upenn.edu/gopher/text/religion/koresh/Koresh%20Log, accessed January 28, 2005. When adults came out, they were dressed in orange prison jump suits, shackled, and paraded before the television cameras. David Koresh was insulted and his religious beliefs belittled in the FBI agents' press conferences.

Stuart A. Wright has demonstrated that FBI negotiators are well aware of the importance of building trust in the subjects with whom they are negotiating, and they are trained in methods to build that trust. He concludes that the negotiations with the Branch Davidians were deliberately sabotaged by FBI agents. After the 1993 conflict at Mount Carmel a disconnect was documented between the efforts of the FBI negotiating team and the methods favored by the tactical team known as the Hostage Rescue Team (HRT) commanded by Dick Rogers. FBI Special Agent in Charge Jeffrey Jamar appeared to be more influenced by Rogers's aggressive approach than the negotiators' trust-building approach. The FBI's own behavioral scientists and finest negotiators protested the aggressive tactical methods and predicted their result would be disastrous loss of life. Stuart A. Wright, "Anatomy of a Government Massacre: Abuses of Hostage-Barricade Protocols during the Waco Standoff," *Terrorism and Political Violence* 11, no. 2 (1999): 39–68; Stuart A. Wright, "A Decade after Waco: Reassessing Crisis Negotiations at Mount Carmel in Light of New Government Disclosures," *Nova Religio: The Journal of Alternative and Emergent Religions* 7, no. 2 (2003): 101–10; House of Representatives, *Investigation*, 55–67.

Despite all the disincentives applied to them, a total of fourteen adults and twenty-one children came out the residence during the siege. Wessinger, *How the Millennium Comes Violently*, 57.

84 Jack Zimmerman was the attorney who represented Steve Schneider.

85 On April 1, 1993, Dr. James Tabor of University of North Carolina, Charlotte, and Dr. J. Phillip Arnold of the Reunion Institute in Houston discussed the biblical prophecies on a KGBS radio program as a means of communicating with David Koresh and the Branch Davidians. Earlier they had offered their services as intermediaries and "worldview trans-lators" to the FBI agents but had been ignored. David had stated in an audiotaped message broadcast on KRLD radio on February 28, "We are now in the Fifth Seal." The Fifth Seal in the book of Revelation in the King James Version of the Bible reads:

And when he had opened the fifth seal, I saw under the altar the souls of them that were slain for the word of God, and for the testimony which they held; and they cried out with a loud voice saying, How long, O Lord, holy and true, dost thou not judge and avenge our blood on them that dwell on earth? And white robes were given unto everyone of them; and it was said unto them, that they should rest yet for a little season, until their fellow servants also and their brethren, that should be killed as they were, should be fulfilled (Rev. 6:9-11).

Six Branch Davidians had died on February 28 as a result of the ATF raid. Drs. Tabor and Arnold recognized that if the Branch Davidians believed they were in the Fifth Seal, they were waiting to see if the federal agents, now the FBI, would kill the rest of the community. Therefore, Tabor and Arnold argued in their April 1 radio broadcast that the waiting period of a "little season" could last years and that David Koresh and the Branch Davidians should come out of Mount Carmel to spread their message of salvation. On April 2 Steve Schneider told negotiators that the Branch Davidians would come out after Passover.

The weeklong Passover holiday ended on April 13. On April 14, David sent out a letter to his attorney, Dick DeGuerin, instructing him to tell the FBI agents that God had given him permission to write down his interpretation of the Seven Seals of Revelation. After he wrote his interpretation of the Seven Seals the Branch Davidians would come out. David believed that this would fulfill the role of the seventh angel holding the "little book" in Revelation 10:2. David wrote in his letter that when the manuscript was given to Tabor and Arnold for safekeeping the Branch Davidians would come out. A negotiation audiotape for April 14 recorded the Branch Davidians cheering in the background when they heard that there was a plan for them to come out.

On April 16 David Koresh reported to FBI negotiators that he had completed his interpretation of the First Seal of Revelation, and the Branch Davidians began requesting wordprocessing equipment to facilitate the production of the manuscript. The wordprocessing equipment was delivered on April 18, and Ruth Riddle typed up David's interpretation of the First Seal. When she escaped the fire on April 19 she carried a floppy disk on which was saved this fragment of David's uncompleted manuscript. Tabor and Gallagher, *Why Waco?* 5, 7, 9–10; Wessinger, *How the Millennium Comes Violently*, 91–94; House of Representatives, *Investigation*, 65. On "worldview translators" see Phillip Lucas, "How Future Wacos Might Be Avoided: Two Proposals," in *From the Ashes: Making Sense of Waco*, ed. James R. Lewis (Lanham, Md.: Rowman & Littlefield, 1994), 209–12. David Koresh's unfinished manuscript is published in the appendix of Tabor and Gallagher, *Why Waco?* 189–211, with commentary by James D. Tabor and J. Phillip Arnold. See the poem taken from this manuscript in the Appendix of this book.

86 Beginning that morning at 6:00 a.m., the tanks inserted CS gas (2-chlorobenzylidene malononitrile), which is actually

a powder, into the building through their booms and FBI agents fired in ferret rounds that emitted the CS. The CS sprayed into the residence by the tanks was mixed with methylene chloride, which evaporates and leaves the CS powder in the air. Methylene chloride causes disorientation, dizziness, and even coma and death. Ferret rounds are projectiles that were shot into the residence that released the CS powder.

CS burns the skin and respiratory passages very intensely causing a great deal of pain. Overexposure to CS can cause the production of so much respiratory swelling and mucus that death by acute bronchopneumonia or asphyxiation could result. Intense exposure to CS can cause first, second, and third degree burns. CS can cause intense allergic reactions and vomiting.

When burned, CS emits toxic hydrogen cyanide and hydrogen chloride fumes; methylene chloride when burned emits toxic phosgene gas. The FBI fired in almost four hundred ferret rounds as well as sprayed liquid CS by the tanks through their booms.

The United States signed a treaty at the Chemical Weapons Convention in Paris in January 1993 agreeing not to use CS gas in warfare.

See Carol Moore, *The Davidian Massacre: Disturbing Questions about Waco Which Must Be Answered* (Franklin, Tenn., and Springfield, Va.: Legacy Communications and Gun Owners Foundation, 1995), 293, 295-96, 364, 388; Hardy and Kimball, *This Is not an Assault*, 264-65, 270-71, 290; House of Representatives, *Investigation*, 70-75.

The plan approved by Attorney General Janet Reno called for the residence to be gassed gradually over forty-eight hours giving the people an opportunity to come out. However, the plan said that if the Branch Davidians fired upon the agents the on-site commanders had the discretion to speed up the assault. Indeed, the agents reported that the Branch Davidians fired upon them early in the assault. The tanks pumped in large amounts of gas in a short time and began driving into the building and dismantling it. A tank drove through the front of the building to the concrete vault where the mothers and small children had taken shelter. The tank operators had been ordered to insert CS gas into the vault, but it is unknown whether they succeeded in doing so. The tank gassed the area in front of the vault from 11:31 to 11:55. Concrete falling from the roof of the vault fell on the mothers and children. See Hardy and Kimball, *This Is not an Assault*, 285, 288–89; Moore, *Davidian Massacre*, 350–52; House of Representatives, *Investigation*, 71–75.

There are different analyses of where and when the fires started. An independent fire examiner noted that a FLIR tape showed that the first fire began at 11:59 a.m. in the gymnasium in the back of the complex as a tank backed out of that area. At 12:07 p.m. fire was visible on the southeast corner second floor bedroom in the front of the building. By 12:08 p.m. the FLIR tape showed fire in the dining room area, and the fire in the gymnasium was much bigger. By 12:09 the fire in the chapel was visible on FLIR. The fires started in at least three areas of the building where the tanks had entered the residence. See Reavis, *Ashes of Waco*, 273; House of Representatives, *Investigation*, 85; Moore, *Davidian Massacre*, 320–21.

The three or four fires quickly became an inferno that killed seventy-six Branch Davidians, including twenty-three children ages fifteen and younger. Seventeen of the children were ages eight and younger. The total number for the children includes the two infants *in utero*. At least seventeen people died from gunshot wounds.

At 12:13 p.m. FBI agents called for fire trucks. Fire engines arrived at the FBI checkpoint half a mile away at 12:34, but were held back by Special Agent in Charge Jeffrey Jamar. From 12:30 to 12:45 tanks with bulldozer blades pushed burning debris into the fire. At 12:41, after the residence was completely burned, the fire fighters were permitted to spray the smoking ashes with water. See Wessinger, *How the Millennium Comes Violently*, 78; Hardy and Kimball, *This Is Not an Assault*, 292–96; aerial photographs of the fire and fire trucks; visuals in Gifford, Grazecki, McNulty, "Waco: The Rules of Engagement."

The soundtrack to FLIR film taken by a plane flying overhead Mount Carmel revealed that at 12:35 p.m. HRT commander Dick Rogers (HR-1) on-site radioed Special Agent in Charge Jeffrey Jamar (HR-2) at the checkpoint that the agents were attempting to get into the buried bus hoping to rescue the children. Jamar replied: "No one else, I hope." By 12:36 Rogers was shouting angrily for fire trucks to be sent to the burning site immediately. See Hardy and Kimball, *This Is not an Assault*, 294–95.

The government alleged that bug tapes revealed that the Branch Davidians spread fuel and started the fires. Surviving Branch Davidians alleged that fuel was spread when the tanks knocked over a propane tank and kerosene lanterns and containers. Graeme Craddock reported in his deposition that he saw someone in the chapel spreading fuel, and that Pablo Cohen yelled that the fuel should be poured outside, not inside the building. Craddock testified that he later heard Mark Wendel shouting from upstairs to light the fire, which was contradicted by Pablo Cohen in the chapel, "Don't light the fire!" Craddock also testified that the tanks knocked over a propane tank. See Moore, *Davidian Massacre*, 361–86; Oral and Videotaped Deposition of Graeme Craddock, October 28, 1999, 1:200–3, 2:245, 254–56, 259, 261–63, 294, 381, 383, 410–11, 426, 429, 430, 438. See also Graeme Craddock's statements in Van Vleet, Novak, Van Vleet, McNulty, "Waco: A New Revelation." Both Mark Wendel and Pablo Cohen died in the fire.

In 1999 after it was revealed that, after six years of denials, FBI agents had fired two pyrotechnic ferret rounds early on the morning of April 19, former Senator John Danforth was appointed Special Counsel by Attorney General Janet Reno to investigate whether federal agents took actions on April 19 to kill the Branch Davidians. Pyrotechnic or "military rounds" heat up and burn a spark to release tear gas, and thus could cause a fire. Although the Danforth Report concluded that these pyrotechnic rounds were not involved in the fire, questions remain about whether federal agents fired pyrotechnic rounds into the back of the building about the time of the fire, or whether they threw flares into the building, which they had brought on site. Television video captured the distinctive white smoke produced by an M-651 pyrotechnic tear gas round at 12:09 p.m. in the back of the building. See Hardy and Kimball, *This Is not an Assault,* 280–82; Lee Hancock, "ATF Attempts to Block Search for Siege Evidence: Judge Acts to Let Rangers Look for Tear-Gas Shell," *Dallas Morning News,* September 4, 1999; Lee Hancock, "Amount of Tear Gas Fired at Waco Siege Questioned: Investigators Say More Pyrotechnic Rounds Suspected," *Dallas Morning News,* March 5, 2000; Danforth, "Final Report."

The video "Waco: A New Revelation" reports that six flash bang (pyrotechnic) grenades were discovered by Michael McNulty in the government's evidence locker relating to this case. They had been mislabeled as gun "silencers." The Texas Rangers report indicated that they had been retrieved from the cafeteria, the chapel, and the front corner of the building, all areas where fires originated. The video also reports that Michael McNulty also found in the evidence locker two 40-mm. pyrotechnic rounds that had been recovered from the rubble at the back of the building.

See Jean E. Rosenfeld, "The Use of the Military at Waco: The Danforth Report in Context," *Nova Religio: The Journal of Alternative and Emergent Religions* 5, no. 1 (2001): 171–85, on the limitations of the Danforth Report. According to Rosenfeld, comparison of the Danforth Report with other government reports on the Branch Davidian case "reveals inconsistencies, errors, omissions, terminology, and interpretations that raise questions about violations of the laws separating the armed forces from civilian police operations against United States citizens on U.S. soil" (171).

Nine Branch Davidians escaped the fire: Renos Avraam (British, 32), Jaime Castillo (Mexican American, 24), Graeme Craddock (European Australian, 35), Clive Doyle (European American, 52), Misty Ferguson (European American, 17), Derek Lovelock (African British, 37), Ruth Riddle (European Canadian, 32), David Thibodeau (European American, 24), Marjorie Thomas (African British, 30). Clive Doyle suffered burns on his hands and ankle; Misty Ferguson was burned on her face and body, and her hands were so severely burned that the fingers had to be amputated; Ruth Riddle suffered a broken ankle and burns; Marjorie Thomas had severe burns all over her body.

87 This was the American *A Current Affair* news magazine program, which aired from 1986 to 1996. See Associated Press, January 13, 2005. It produced a report on the Branch Davidians in 1987 after the shootout with George Roden. Subsequently, *A Current Affair* did a report on Bonnie Haldeman.

88 David died of a gunshot wound to the forehead and also suffered from inhalation of smoke and carbon monoxide as well as massive charring of the body. David is buried in a cemetery in Tyler, Texas. See "Autopsy of David Koresh," at <http://www.public-action.com/SkyWriter/WacoMuseum/death/8/8_aut.html>, accessed January 8, 2006.

The young children and their mothers died inside the concrete room that was a vault in the earlier Administration Building on that site and which the federal agents called "the bunker." When the Administration Building burned down in 1983 the vault was the only structure that survived the fire and none of the papers and records inside the vault had burned. When the large residence was built at Mount Carmel, the vault served as a storage area next to the kitchen and a walk-in refrigerator was placed there. Sometime in 1992 David Koresh stored the weapons and ammunitions in part of the vault.

The mothers and young children in the vault died from suffocation, smoke inhalation, inhalation of carbon monoxide, gunshot wounds, and one stab wound. David Hardy has alleged that when a tank drove through the back of the building to the vault that it inserted CS gas directly into the vault. He cites a radio command given at 10:57 a.m. by HRT commander Dick Rogers to direct delivery of the CS gas to the base of the central tower, i.e. the vault. The government disputes the allegation that CS gas was placed directly inside the vault, and the congressional report cites expert reports stating that even if CS gas and the accompanying dispersant, methylene chloride, were sprayed into the vault through the tank's boom the amount of these chemicals inside the room would not have been lethal. However, the anaesthetic and disorientation effect of the methyene chloride could have impaired attempts to escape the room. Doyle Tape #22, interview with Clive Doyle on November 27, 2004, at Mount Carmel; List of Autopsy Reports Provided by Justice of Peace, McLennan County, Precinct 2, http://public-action.com/SkyWriter/WacoMuseum/death/map/d_list00.html, accessed August 8, 2006; Hardy and Kimball, *This Is not an Assault*, 288–90; House of Representatives, *Investigation into the Activities*, 72–75.

89 Federal Judge Walter Smith Jr. presided over the criminal trial of eleven Branch Davidians held in San Antonio. The Branch Davidians were charged with conspiracy to murder

federal agents, murder of federal agents, and weapons charges. The jury found all of the Branch Davidians on trial innocent of conspiracy to murder federal agents and innocent of murder of federal agents. Clive Doyle, Woodrow Kendrick, and Norman Allison were found innocent of all charges.

At the last minute in the trial, the defense attorneys, without consulting their clients, permitted the jury's consideration of charges of manslaughter, defined by the judge as unlawfully killing in "the sudden heat of passion caused by adequate provocation" (Reavis, *Ashes of Waco*, 295). The jury, as reported later, by the forewoman Sarah Bain, decided to convict some of the Branch Davidians of manslaughter to indicate that the Branch Davidians were acting in self-defense and that fault was with the ATF agents as well as the Branch Davidians. The jury members believed that the manslaughter verdict would carry a lighter penalty and that the convicted Branch Davidians would be released for the time they had already served in prison.

The jury found seven of the defendants guilty of aiding and abetting voluntary manslaughter of federal agents, five of them additionally guilty of carrying a firearm during the commission of a crime of violence, and Paul Fatta and Graeme Craddock were found guilty of arms violations. Subsequently Judge Walter Smith imposed a guilty verdict for conspiracy to murder federal agents on five of the defendants and gave them lengthy sentences: Renos Avraam, Brad Branch, Jaime Castillo, Livingstone Fagan, and Kevin Whitecliff were sentenced to forty years.

Since Graeme Craddock's own testimony indicated that he had possession of a weapon during the ATF shootout, he was sentenced to twenty years. Ruth Riddle was sentenced to five years for possessing a weapon during the shootout. Paul Fatta, who handled much of the Branch Davidian gun dealing and who was not present at Mount Carmel during the shootout, was sentenced to fifteen years for weapons violations.

All of the defendents were fined in amounts from $2,000 to $50,000, and they were required to pay $1,200,000 in restitution.

Kathy Schroeder, after being charged with participating in the gunfight, cooperated with the prosecution by providing testimony, and later received a sentence of three years.

The forty-year sentences were appealed to the Supreme Court, which ruled in 2000 that the sentences were excessive and sent the case back to Judge Smith. Judge Smith then sentenced Renos Avraam, Brad Branch, Jaime Castillo, Livingstone Fagan, and Kevin Whitecliff to fifteen years.

Reavis, *Ashes of Waco*, 278–300; James T. Richardson, "'Showtime' in Texas: Social Production of the Branch Davidian Trials," *Nova Religio: The Journal of Alternative and Emergent Religions* 5, no. 1 (2001): 152–70; Moore, *Davidian Massacre*, 444–45; Tommy Witherspoon, "Doing Time: Branch Davidians Still Behind Bars Display Hope, Anguish," *Waco Tribune-Herald*, March 6, 2003, <http://www.wacotrib.com/news/content/coxnet/branchdavidian/0306_hope.html>, now defunct.

Renos Avraam, Brad Branch, Jaime Castillo, Kevin Whitecliff, Graeme Craddock, and Paul Fatta were released from prison in 2006. Renos Avraam, a British citizen, and Graeme Craddock, an Australian citizen, were deported to their respective countries. Brad Branch, Jaime Castillo, Kevin Whitecliff, and Paul Fatta were serving probation in the United States. Livingstone Fagan was released in May 2007, and deported to Britain.

The former Branch Davidian prisoners are forbidden to meet with each other, since it is illegal for convicted felons to associate with one another. As a condition of their probations, Branch, Castillo, Fatta, and Whitecliff were told that they also could not associate with their co-defendants, which meant that they could not meet with Clive Doyle, Norman Allison, Woodrow Kendrick, Kathy Schroeder, and Ruth Riddle. Apparently the federal agents were singling out Clive Doyle as someone with whom the paroled men could not associate, thereby effectively preventing the revival of a group of Koresh Branch Davidians at Mount Carmel or elsewhere in the United States. Personal communications from Clive Doyle, Paul Fatta, and Jaime Castillo in July 2006.

90 Branch Davidian survivors and relatives of deceased Branch Davidians filed a $675 million wrongful death lawsuit against the federal government. In 2000 it came to trial in Waco in Judge Walter Smith Jr.'s court. Attorneys Michael Caddell and Cynthia Chapman represented the families suing on behalf of many of the deceased children. Ramsey Clark, former Attorney General under President Lyndon B. Johnson, represented the surviving Branch Davidians. David Hardy was part of the team of attorneys working with Ramsey Clark. Jim Brannon represented a smaller number of estates of deceased Branch Davidian children. The plaintiffs' attorneys asked that Judge Smith recuse himself from conducting the trial and that another judge be appointed because of alleged bias against the Branch Davidians manifested in the 1994 criminal trial. Judge Smith declined to recuse himself, but elected to appoint an advisory jury in the civil trial. See Hardy and Kimball, *This Is not an Assault*, 133–34; Richardson, "'Showtime' in Texas," 162–63.

During the civil trial, defense attorneys asked for and were granted "discretionary function immunity" for many of the federal agents' activities in 1993 in relation to the Branch Davidians. According to James T. Richardson, discretionary function immunity is the concept that "a law enforcement officer in the course of his or her duty must make decisions, sometimes quickly, and that second-guessing those decisions is not to be allowed, and that the government is not to be held liable for the outcome of such decisions made in good faith in the heat of the moment" (Richardson, "'Showtime' in Texas," 169 n. 42). Judge Smith's decision to grant discretionary function immunity according to Richardson:

Limited the time frame of the case to the 51-day siege, and did not allow presentations of evidence of the decision-making process and actions that led up to the initial BATF raid or about the decision-making processes used by the FBI and the Justice Department that led to the assault on 19 April 1993. Thus the jury did not hear about misrepresentations by BATF officials that drugs were being manufactured at Mount Carmel Center, a false claim which allowed them access to government material and training. They also did not hear about a number of other issues of questionable judgment, such as the decision to proceed with the initial BATF raid after the element of surprise was lost and the Davidians learned that the BATF officials were coming. The jury did not hear, as well, much evidence about the misrepresentations to newly appointed Attorney General Janet Reno about the use of deadly CS gas. Her agreement to the plan outlined by the FBI, which included using the gas (albeit differently than what was actually done), was a major event that could not be fully explored given the judge's rulings (163).

According to Richardson, "discretion" exercised by a judge refers to the independent decisions a judge makes in deciding what evidence can and cannot be presented to a jury and the instructions a judge gives to a jury about the matters to be decided. Richardson argues that the discretion exercised by Judge Smith in the 1994 criminal trial and the 2000 civil trial greatly affected the outcome in each. Richardson describes trials as "social productions," which in the case of the Branch Davidians, were designed to stigmatize and degrade the Branch Davidians and thereby reinforce the correctness of the activities of federal agents at Mount Carmel and thus protect them from criminal charges in the case (152–57).

Sociologist Stuart Wright, who observed the 2000 civil trial, reports that Judge Smith restricted presentation of evidence to the fifty-one days between the ATF raid on February 28, 1993 and the fire on April 19, 1993. The jury was asked to decide whether the ATF agents used excessive force in delivering the warrants on February 28, but they were not presented with evidence about the decision-making processes of the ATF prior to the raid. The jury was asked to determine whether FBI agents took actions that caused the deaths of Branch Davidians on April 19, but Judge Smith's exercise of discretion prevented the jury from hearing evidence about the FBI's decision to abandon negotiations ten days into the standoff and implement a policy of "stress escalation" by shining bright spotlights at the residence during the night, blasting the Branch Davidians with irritating sounds exceeding a hundred and five decibels, threatening the Branch Davidians by maneuvers and destruction of property by the tanks, and sending mixed messages to the Branch Davidians by the conciliatory communications from the negotiators and the aggressive and destructive actions on the part of the tactical team. The jury never got to hear evidence that successful negotiations strategies are well known to be based on trust-building and that the stress escalation program carried out by the FBI demolished any trust the negotiators managed to elicit from the Branch Davidians. Furthermore the FBI's stress escalation strategy bonded the Branch Davidians together more strongly as an apocalyptic community committed to the interpretations of the Bible's prophecies by their messiah David Koresh. Lastly the jury was not allowed to consider evidence about the FBI's decision to utilize CS gas. See Stuart A. Wright, "Justice Denied: The Waco Civil Trial," *Nova Religio: Journal of Alternative and Emergent Religions* 5, no. 1 (2001): 143–51.

In the Branch Davidian civil trial, the advisory jury took two and one-half hours to decide that the government was not guilty of causing the Branch Davidians' deaths in 1993 and that the Branch Davidians caused the fire. Richardson, "'Showtime' in Texas," 162.

91 Unexpectedly, on November 11, 2005 Bill Clinton, speaking at a conference at Hofstra University, stated that the Branch Davidian case was one of the biggest failures of his presidency. He said:

I think we made a mistake letting the forces go into Waco [Mount Carmel] instead of waiting them out, and I will always regret that. This is another thing you need to analyze as President: When do you take your experts' advice and when do you do what you think is right? How do you know when to follow your gut and when do you listen to others? I think the answer is when your gut feels strong, and when it's an area you know something too. If you're blind ignorant then you ought to listen to someone else, and if you don't have a real strong feeling. I had a real strong feeling. I dealt with problems like Waco when I was Governor and we should have waited them out. Janet Reno was new on the job. She got enormous pressure from the FBI to go ahead and go in there. And *I* am responsible for that, because I told her if that's what they want to do and she thought it was right. It was a mistake and I am responsible. And that's not one of those things you get A for effort on.

A video of Clinton's speech is at http://www.hofstra.edu/CampusL/Culture/culture_clinton_video_archive.cfm. Nancy Ross and Deborah Green sent out an email about Clinton's statements on November 29, 2005.

Bill Clinton is referring above to the siege of a militant extreme rightwing Christian group that was harboring fugitives from the law, called the Covenant, Sword, and the Arm of the Lord, that occurred when he was governor of Arkansas. The FBI's Hostage Rescue Team, then led by Danny Coulson, successfully negotiated a surrender with no bloodshed by taking a low-key tactical presence and utilizing innovative negotiation techniques. See Kerry Noble, *Tabernacle of Hate: Why They Bombed Oklahoma City* (Prescott, Ont.: Voyageur Publishing, 1998); Danny O. Coulson and Elaine Shannon, *No Heroes: Inside the FBI's Secret Counter-Terror Force* (New York: Pocket Books, 1999), 209–92.

92　Bonnie is speaking in 2004.

93　Bonnie Haldeman, Clive Doyle, and Sheila and Kimberly Martin came to New Orleans in February 2003 to hear Michael Caddell and Ramsey Clark argue in the United States 5th Circuit Court of Appeals for another civil trial on the grounds that Judge Walter Smith Jr. was biased against the Branch Davidians. The judges of the 5th Circuit Court of Appeals subsequently denied the appeal. See Bruce Nolan, "Davidian Faith, Pain Living On," Religion News Service, February 15, 2003; Associated Press, "Court Rejects Davidian Claim against the U.S.," July 15, 2003.

94　In 2004 the Supreme Court declined to hear the appeal of the Branch Davidians in the civil case alleging bias on the part of Judge Walter Smith Jr. Associated Press, "High Court Declines to Hear Suits over Judge," March 23, 2004.

95　Bonnie makes a point of giving interviews whenever she is asked. Her purpose is to humanize her deceased loved ones and friends.

96 Charles Pace, a Branch Davidian going back to the days of Ben and Lois Roden, sees David Koresh as a false prophet who misled the elders of the church. Conversation with Charles Pace on April 19, 2003 at Mount Carmel.

97 · The museum called "Visitors' Center" contained a model of the residence that burned in 1993, photographs of the ATF agents and the Branch Davidians who died, photographs of the ATF raid and the fire, and lastly, FBI "trophy photos" of agents posing triumphantly, and even flexing their muscles, over the ashes of the residence where little red flags marked the location of each body. The trophy photos also show how on April 19, 1993 the ATF raised three flags over the burned residence: the American flag, the state of Texas flag, and the ATF flag. These trophy photos were provided to the Branch Davidians by their attorneys in the criminal trial. The museum was closed and its contents removed for safekeeping when Clive Doyle moved off the Mount Carmel property in March 2006.

98 The chapel is built on the site of the residence that burned in 1993, but it is much smaller. April 19, 2006 was the first time the surviving Branch Davidians held the memorial off the Mount Carmel property.

99 Dick DeGuerin and Jack Zimmerman testified before the 1994 congressional hearings. They went into Mount Carmel several times (DeGuerin five times, Zimmerman twice) during the siege and examined the bullet holes in the doors, walls and ceiling. They testified that the majority of the holes were made by bullets entering from the outside. Jack Zimmerman, a Marine Corps Reserve colonel and former combat artillery officer, testified in the 1994 criminal trial, that the holes in the ceilings were made by bullets fired from above and therefore must have been shot from the helicopters. See Reavis, *Ashes of Waco*, 134, 142, 252. To view part of their congressional testimony see "Waco: The Rules of Engagement." Also see

"Statement of Dick DeGuerin, Attorney for David Koresh,"
22–101; "Statement of Jack Zimmerman, Attorney for Steve
Schneider," 19–21; "Prepared Statement of Dick DeGuerin,
Lawyer for David Koresh," 102–28; "Prepared Statement of
Jack B. Zimmerman, Attorney for Steve Schneider," 129–41,
in House of Representatives, *Activities of Federal Law Enforcement Agents, Part 2.*

100   In March 2006 Clive Doyle moved off of the Mount Carmel
property to an apartment in Waco. Charles Pace promptly
exerted control over the property. He cut down the crape
myrtle tree dedicated to David Koresh. He moved the memorial stones containing the names of the deceased Branch
Davidians from under the trees planted for each person who
died in 1993.

On April 19, 2006 the surviving Branch Davidians gathered with friends at a restaurant in Waco to remember their
deceased loved ones. Before joining the friends at the restaurant, Bonnie Haldeman and David Koresh's father, Bobby
Howell, went out to Mount Carmel to witness the memorial
service planned by Charles Pace. Upon learning that Charles
Pace intended to burn ceremonially the branches from David
Koresh's crape myrtle tree, Bonnie and Bobby gathered up
the branches, put them in the back of Bobby's pickup truck,
and left. The Pace group then resorted to burning the remaining roots of David Koresh's tree. Back at the restaurant, Bonnie told a *Waco Tribune-Herald* reporter, "It's just a friggin'
tree, but it's a symbol." See Cindy V. Culp, "Branch Davidians Caught in Yet Another Power Struggle," *Waco Tribune-
Herald*, April 20, 2006, http://www.cesnur.org/2006/waco.
htm#Anchor-Controversia-13910.

For the foreseeable future, the Branch Davidians will be
holding their memorial gatherings on April 19 some place
else besides the Mount Carmel property.

101 Timothy McVeigh, a Gulf War veteran, visited the area of Mount Carmel in 1993 during the siege. He was angered at the actions the government agents were taking against the Branch Davidians. During his trial for the Oklahoma City bombing of the Murrah federal building, which killed 168 people including nineteen children, McVeigh's attorney presented evidence that McVeigh was incensed at the treatment of the Branch Davidians by federal agents. McVeigh was executed on June 11, 2001. See Lou Michel and Dan Herbeck, *American Terrorist: Timothy McVeigh and the Oklahoma City Bombing* (New York: ReganBooks 2001), 118-20, 135–41, 168, 179, 379–80; CNN, "McVeigh Defense Focuses on Waco Rage," CNN Interactive, June 10, 1997, http://www.cnn.com/US/9706/10/mcveigh/#3.

102 In 1995 a crape myrtle tree was planted at Mount Carmel for each Branch Davidian who died in 1993. After Sheila Martin's son Jamie died in 1998 from complications due to his health challenges resulting from the meningitis he contracted when he was a baby, a tree was planted there for Jamie Martin also.

103 The ownership of the Mount Carmel property can be disputed by the Koresh Branch Davidians in the future. It has never been settled who the legal heirs of the trustees of the General Assocation of the Branch Davidian Seventh-day Adventists are. On January 19, 1973 Ben Roden executed a warranty deed selling the property for $1.00 to Ben L. Roden, Lois I. Roden, and George Roden, as trustees of "The Branch Davidian Seventh-day Adventists, an Association constituting a Church." There are numerous irregularities in the transactions relating to the Mount Carmel property. For one, this warranty deed is for 941.69 acres and not the actual 77.86 acres. The Pace Branch Davidian group will not be able to claim exclusive ownership of the property

unless rival Branch Davidians do not contest its control of the property for ten years. Personal communications from attorney Richard Ruppert.

104 Mount Carmel currently does not have access to city water. The well at Mount Carmel was destroyed in 1993.

105 In 2004–2007 Ofelia Santoyo lived at Mount Carmel in Charles Pace's Branch Davidian community.

106 There were about 123 people inside Mount Carmel immediately after the ATF raid on February 28, 1993. This number is not counting Branch Davidians living nearby, those who had left the property earlier that morning, and those living in California. See Tabor and Gallagher, *Why Waco?* 3.

107 Joshua Sylvia (European American) is the son of Stan and Lorraine ("Larry") Sylvia. Joshua (7 in 1993) was sent out during the siege. His father was at the Branch Davidians' house in Pomona, California. His mother, Larry Sylvia (40), and his sisters, Rachel (12) and Hollywood (1), died in the fire.

108 One of the allegations made by some former members was that David administered severe spankings to very young children. To date the surviving children of Mount Carmel, now young people, have not verified this.

A 1994 article by clinical-child psychologist Larry Lilliston asks, "Who Committed Child Abuse at Waco?" He points out that federal agents, claiming to want to protect the children, subjected them to danger and terror by the ATF shootout, deprivation of food, water, and a clean environment by the siege, during which they experienced the high decibel sounds and bright lights of the psychological warfare, and then subjected them to a terrifying CS gas and tank assault as the building around them was dismantled and they finally died in the fire. Larry Lilliston, "Who Committed Child Abuse at Waco?" in Lewis, *From the Ashes*, 169–73.

109 Catherine Matteson explained that David's imperfections and life experiences meant that he understood sin and therefore understood the human condition. Since God is perfect

and Jesus Christ was perfect they do not have an understanding of humanity's sinful nature. Christ returned as a sinful messiah, David Koresh, in order to understand what sin is about. This is important in Branch Davidian theology, because the Branch Davidians believe that David, as the resurrected Endtime Christ, will bring judgment to humanity. Catherine emphasized that although David was sinful, he was also righteous, because he obeyed God. Interview with Catherine Matteson on August 15, 2003 in Waco, Texas.

110   Livingstone Fagan (African British, 34 in 1993) was an Adventist lay minister and studying for his master's degree in theology at Newbold College in Nottingham when he heard David give a talk in 1988. According to Livingstone as reported in David Thibodeau's book, "I heard a couple of his studies, and in three hours I perceived more biblical truths than I had done the entire eight years I'd been involved with organized religion. It was clear to me that David offered a highly intelligent, systematic inquiry into the nature of Scripture." Thibodeau and Whiteson, *A Place Called Waco*, 32–33.

   Livingstone Fagan was sent out of Mount Carmel during the siege to serve as David's theological spokesman, but he was put in jail. He was convicted in the 1994 criminal trial, and was released in May 2007 and deported to England. From prison, Livingstone produced several theological essays. Livingstone's mother, Doris (60), and wife, Evette (30), died in the fire. Their two children, Nehara (4 in 1993) and Renea (7 in 1993), were sent out during the siege.

111   Kathy Andrade was twenty-four when she died in the fire with her daughter by David, Chanel (1). Her sister, Jennifer Andrade, was 19 when she died in the fire.

112   Graeme Craddock, in his deposition, said about David's ability to interpret the biblical prophecies:

[T]he reason why I came to Mount Carmel, the reason why I stayed, is because, to my mind, David Koresh was able to put this Bible together better than anyone else; and that's something I can't explain to anyone else. You had to have been there to have seen. It took him weeks to do but once you saw where he was getting at, saw the evidence in the book, what he was trying to explain, then you were, you were hooked and you had to stay.

Oral and Videotaped Deposition of Graeme Craddock, October 28, 1999.

113 James D. Tabor, e-mail to Catherine Wessinger dated September 4, 2006.

114 (Gladewater, Tex.: GMC Records, 1996).

115 Wessinger, *How the Millennium Comes Violently*, 75–77; Tabor and Gallagher, *Why Waco?* David Koresh's unfinished manuscript can be read in full in Tabor and Gallagher, *Why Waco?* 191–203. Permission to reprint this poem is given by James Tabor in an e-mail dated 4 September 2006 to Catherine Wessinger.

WORKS CITED

9-1-1 audiotapes. 1993. February 28.

Associated Press. 2003. "Court Rejects Davidian Claim against the U.S." July 15.

———. 2004. "High Court Declines to Hear Suits over Judge." March 23.

Breault, Marc, and Martin King. 1993. *Inside the Cult: A Member's Chilling, Exclusive Account of Madness and Depravity in David Koresh's Compound.* New York: Signet Books.

CNN. 1997. "McVeigh Defense Focuses on Waco Rage." CNN Interactive. June 10. <http://www.cnn.com/US/9706/10/mcveigh/#3>.

Craddock, Graeme. 1999. Oral and Videotaped Deposition of Graeme Craddock, October 28. *Isabel G. Andrade et al. v. Phillip J. Cojnacki et al.,* United States District Court for the Western District of Texas, Waco Division, No. W-96-CA-139.

Culp, Cindy V. 2006. "Branch Davidians Caught in Yet Another Power Struggle." *Waco Tribune-Herald*. April 20. <http://www.cesnur.org/2006/waco.htm#Anchor-Con-troversia-13910>.

Danforth, John, Special Council. 2000. "Final Report to the Deputy Attorney General Concerning the 1993 Confrontation at the Mt. Carmel Complex, Waco, Texas, November 8, 2000 Pursuant to Order No. 2256-99 of the Attorney General." Available at <http://www.apolo-geticsindex.org/pdf/finalreport.pdf>.

Docherty, Jayne Seminare. 2001. *Learning the Lessons from Waco: When the Parties Bring Their Gods to the Negotiation Table*. Syracuse: Syracuse University Press.

Doyle, Clive. 2004. Tape #22. Interview with Clive Doyle at Mount Carmel Center on November 27.

———. 2004. Tape #24. Interview with Clive Doyle at Mount Carmel Center on November 27.

———. 2005. Newsletter for the General Association of the Branch Davidian Seventh Day Adventists. March.

Dratt, Jude, and Jennifer Lew Goldstone, producers. 2003. *Primetime: Witness: The Children of Waco*. New York: ABC News. Television broadcast April 17.

Faubion, James. 2001. *The Lights and Shadows of Waco: Millennialism Today*. Princeton: Princeton University Press.

Gallagher, Eugene V. 2000. " 'Theology Is Life and Death': David Koresh on Violence, Persecution, and the Millennium." In *Millennialism, Persecution, and Violence: Historical Cases*, ed. Catherine Wessinger, 82–100. Syracuse: Syracuse University Press.

Gifford, Dan, William Gazecki, and Michael McNulty, producers. 1997. "Waco: The Rules of Engagement." Los Angeles: Fifth Estate Productions.

Haldeman, Bonnie. 2004. Tape #3. Interview with Bonnie Haldeman and Clive Doyle in Chandler, Texas on July 2.

Hancock, Lee. 1999. "ATF Attempts to Block Search for Siege Evidence: Judge Acts to Let Rangers Look for Tear-Gas Shell," *Dallas Morning News*, September 4.

———. 2000. "Amount of Tear Gas Fired at Waco Siege Questioned: Investigators Say More Pyrotechnic Rounds Suspected," *Dallas Morning News*, March 5.

Hardy, David T., with Rex Kimball. 2001. *This Is not an Assault: Penetrating the Web of Official Lies Regarding the Waco Incident*. N.p.: Xlibris Corporation.

House of Representatives. 1996. *Activities of Federal Law Enforcement Agencies toward the Branch Davidians (Part 1): Joint Hearings Before the Subcommittee on Crime of the Committee on the Judiciary, House of Representatives, and the Subcommittee on National Security, International Affairs, and Criminal Justice of the Committee on Government Reform and Oversight, One Hundred Fourth Congress, First Session, July 19, 20, 21, and 24, 1995. Committee on the Judiciary Serial No. 72*. Washington, D.C.: U.S. Government Printing Office.

———. 1996. *Activities of Federal Law Enforcement Agencies toward the Branch Davidians (Part 2): Joint Hearings before the Subcommittee on Crime of the Committee on the Judiciary, House of Representatives, and the Subcommittee on National Security, International Affairs, and Criminal Justice of the Committee on Government Reform and Oversight, One Hundred Fourth Congress, First Session, July 25, 26, and 27, 1995. Committee on the Judiciary Serial No. 72*. Washington, D.C.: U.S. Government Printing Office.

——. 1996. *Investigation into the Activities of Federal Law Enforcement Agencies toward the Branch Davidians: Thirteenth Report by the Committee on Government Reform and Oversight Prepared in Conjunction with the Committee on the Judiciary together with Additional and Dissenting Views*. Washington, D.C.: U.S. Government Printing Office.

Koresh, David. 1993. KRLD interview, April 19. Audiotape.

——. 1993. March 2 audiotape.

——. 1996. *Songs to Grandpa*. Gladewater, Tex.: GMC Records. Audiotape.

"Judgment." 2000. *Trustees of the Branch Davidian Seventh-day Adventists Association v. George Buchanan Roden and Amo Bishop Roden et al.*, District Court of McLennan County, Texas, 74th Judicial District, No. 96-1152-3.

Justice of the Peace, McLennan County, Precinct 2. 2005. List of Autopsy Reports. <http://www.public-action.com/SkyWriter/WacoMuseum/death/map/d_list00.html>.

Lilliston, Larry. 1994. "Who Committed Child Abuse at Waco?" In *From the Ashes: Making Sense of Waco*, edited by James R. Lewis, 169–73. Lanham, Md.: Rowman & Littlefield.

Lucas, Phillip. 1994. "How Future Wacos Might Be Avoided: Two Proposals." In *From the Ashes: Making Sense of Waco*, ed. James R. Lewis, 209–12. Lanham, Md.: Rowman & Littlefield.

Martin, Sheila. 2004. Tape #2B. Interview with Sheila Martin in Fort Worth, Texas on October 10.

Matteson, Catherine. 2003. Interview on August 15 in Waco, Texas.

——. 2004. Tape #2. Interview with Catherine Matteson in Waco, Texas on October 11.

——. 2004. Tape #3. Interview with Catherine Matteson in Waco, Texas on November 26.

——. 2004. Tape #4. Interview with Catherine Matteson in Waco, Texas on November 26.

McNulty, Michael, producer. 2001. "The F.L.I.R. Project." Fort Collins, Colo.: COPS Productions.

Michel, Lou, and Dan Herbeck. 2001. *American Terrorist: Timothy McVeigh and the Oklahoma City Bombing.* New York: ReganBooks.

Moore, Carol. 1995. *The Davidian Massacre: Disturbing Questions about Waco Which Must Be Answered.* Franklin, Tenn., and Springfield, Va.: Legacy Communications and Gun Owners Foundation.

Nolan, Bruce. 2003. "Davidian Faith, Pain Living On." Religion News Service, February 15.

Reavis. Dick J. 1995. *The Ashes of Waco: An Investigation.* New York: Simon & Schuster.

Richardson, James T. 2001. "'Showtime' in Texas: Social Production of the Branch Davidian Trials." *Nova Religio: The Journal of Alternative and Emergent Religions* 5, no. 1: 152–70.

Robertson, J. J. 1996. *Beyond the Flames: This Is the True Story of the Massacre at Waco.* San Diego: J. J. Robertson.

Roden, Amo Paul Bishop. 2004. "Original Petition and Complaint." *Amo Paul Bishop Roden v. Clive Doyle and the McLennan County Sheriff's Department*, District Court of McLennan County, Texas, 74th Judicial District, No. 2004-3493-3.

Rosenfeld, Jean E. 2001. "The Use of the Military at Waco: The Danforth Report in Context." *Nova Religio: The Journal of Alternative and Emergent Religions* 5, no. 1: 171–85.

Samples, Kenneth, Erwin de Castro, Richard Abanes, and Robert Lyle. 1994. *Prophets of the Apocalypse: David Koresh and Other American Messiahs*. Grand Rapids: Baker Books, 1994.

Schroeder, Kathryn. 1999. "Oral Deposition of Kathryn Schroeder, August 30, 1999." *Isabel G. Andrade, et al v. Phillip J. Chojnacki, et al, and United States of America*, United States District Court, Western District of Texas, Waco Division, Civil Action No. W 96 CA 139.

Tabor, James. [2004.] "David Koresh and the Branch Davidians." <http://www.pbs.org/wgbh/pages/frontline/shows/apocalypse/explaination/cults.html>. Accessed February 6.

——. 2005. "David Koresh." *Encyclopedia of Religion*. 2d ed. Detroit: Thomson Gale: 8:5237-39.

——. [2005.] "The Events at Waco: An Interpretative Log." <http://ccat.sas.upenn.edu/gopher/text/religion/Koresh%20Log>. Accessed January 28.

Tabor, James D., and Eugene V. Gallagher. 1995. *Why Waco? Cults and the Battle for Religious Freedom in America*. Berkeley: University of California Press.

Thibodeau, David, and Leon W. Whiteson. 1999. *A Place Called Waco: A Survivor's Story*. New York: Public Affairs.

Van Vleet, Rick, Stephen M. Novak, Jason Van Vleet, and Michael McNulty, producers. 1999. "Waco: A New Revelation." MGA Films, Inc.

Wessinger, Catherine. 2000. *How the Millennium Comes Violently: From Jonestown to Heaven's Gate*. New York: Seven Bridges Press. Available at <http://www.loyno.edu/~wessing>.

——. 2005. "Autobiographies of Three Surviving Branch Davidians: An Initial Report." *Fieldwork in Religion* 1, no. 2: 165–97.

——. 2006. "The Branch Davidians and Religion Reporting: A Ten-Year Retrospective." In *Expecting the End: Millennialism in Social and Historical Context*, edited by Kenneth G. C. Newport and Crawford Gribben, 147–72, 270–74. Waco: Baylor University Press.

Witherspoon, Tommy. 2003. "Doing Time: Branch Davidians Still Behind Bars Display Hope, Anguish." *Waco Tribune-Herald*. March 6.

Wright, Stuart A. 1999. "Anatomy of a Government Massacre: Abuses of Hostage-Barricade Protocols during the Waco Standoff." *Terrorism and Political Violence* 11, no. 2: 39–68.

——. 2001. "Justice Denied: The Waco Civil Trial." *Nova Religio: The Journal of Alternative and Emergent Religions* 5, no. 1: 143–51.

——. 2003. "A Decade after Waco: Reassessing Crisis Negotiations at Mount Carmel in Light of New Government Disclosures." *Nova Religio: The Journal of Alternative and Emergent Religions* 7, no. 2: 101–10.

INDEX